I Live Next Door to my Neighbor

Deborah Todaro Parsons

Illustrated by: Stacy A. Karnes

Burdock Acres
Farwell, MI

Copyright © 2000 by Burdock Acres

All rights reserved. No part of this book may be reproduced or transmitted in any form or by any means, electronic or mechanical, including photo-copying, recording, or by any information storage and retrieval system, without permission in writing from the publisher.

Published by Burdock Acres
11023 N. Whiteville
Farwell, MI 48622

Publisher's Cataloging-in Publication Data
Parsons, Deborah Todaro
   I live next door to my neighbor / Deborah Todaro Parsons; illustrated by Stacy A. Karnes - Farwell, MI: Burdock Acres, 2000.
       p.   cm.
   ISBN 0-9678049-0-6

   1. Parsons, Deborah Todaro. 2. Bus drivers -- United States -- Anecdotes. I. Title.
TL232.3 .P37   2000   99-068798
388.3/22044/092   dc21   CIP

PROJECT COORDINATION BY JENKINS GROUP, INC.

03 02 01 00 ▲ 5 4 3 2 1

Printed in the United States of America

Dedication

This book is dedicated to my mother, Patricia Ann Todaro. Mom, you have always been able to show me the humor in everyday life through your "joke of the day" and the way you view the world. So, this is for you, My Mom. Thank you for your laughter.

Acknowledgments

Without all of the people who helped me with this book, it would not have ever left the little pieces of paper that it was scratched down on.

This may seem like an awful long list but some people need more help than others and I am one of them.

To my husband of twenty-five years, thank you for your faith and your endless love.

To my three boys Dennis, James, and Michael who are the greatest achievements of my life.

To Doctor Daniel Fachting, Mary Jo Fachting, and Amy Fachting who spent weeks on the book correcting my grammar and trying to figure out if I was using English. Thank you.

A thank you to my boss George Bradley, one of the greatest men I may ever know.

To all my family who has put up with my humor and teasing for years. Thank you.

To the many people who read, corrected, and let me rattle on about my ideas a very big thank you to: Janet Clement, Julie Baltrus, Kristy Baltrus, Patti Birchmyer, Karin Leposky, Mary Fancon, Char Smock, Bertha Mae Stough, Phyllis Whitehead, Julie, Isaac, Judy Heimlich, Janis Lowery, Peggy Severance, Lois Rutter, Barb Gibis, John Colosky, Paul Archbold, Tom Peek, Caroline Bradley, Arlyn DeBoer, Lorri Siems, Karin Pomeroy and Dawn Iley.

Thank you to Perry and Dina Emmons for all the extra help, and Dina who has enough stories to write a book of her own.

To Mary Baltrus and Jo Ann Powell, your help was always there.

Thank you to Al White for your endless help and for laughing out loud.

A special thanks to all the children who have ridden on my bus since 1980, especially the children mentioned in this book, thank you for being yourselves and letting me share a little part of each of you.

And above all thank you to God for with out him I would not have needed this list.

To Kyle Ackerman, Abi Armentrout, Jacob Barlow, Whitney Bruner, Kathy Burrill, Kaelynn Carson, Diane Clark, Nick Clark, Matthew Clement, John Cowles, Heather Cowles, Raquel Davis, Lacy Ellison, Andrew Emery, Jasmine Emery, Gaby Fachting, Kylie Fancon, Tim Gariglio, Megan Johnson, Jessica Keenoy, T.J. Kistler, Ashley King, Hope King, Kerry Koontz, Nichole Leineke, Jessica Leineke, Danielle Magnus, D.J. Mann, Chelsea Nevills, Hunter Russo, Ben Schmidt, Steven Schunk, Elizabeth Strouse, Trista Turner, Ty Turner, Tammi Turner, Michelle Turner, Justin Wentworth, Tyler Wentworth, Tommy Whitfield, Justin Wilkerson.

Contents

Training _____ 1
With these directions _____ 5
Argue that one _____ 9
Sick kids _____ 13
Baby sitter _____ 15
Beware of kids bearing gifts _____ 19
No eating on bus until further notice _____ 23
Missing teeth _____ 31
Two thousand crawly things _____ 35
When you gotta go _____ 41
Almost have it right _____ 47
You'll have that _____ 51
Lester _____ 55
School pictures _____ 57
Love and best friends _____ 61
Kids say and do _____ 65
Muddy puddles _____ 73
Slightly stressed _____ 77
Back packs _____ 81

Introduction

We moved to northern Michigan about twenty years ago from a town that was expanding way too fast for us. My husband's family bought a farm and it looked like the perfect place to raise our three boys. So, with a little coaxing, the promise of a new country home and more time together, we decided to try it.

In reality, we spent even less time together, milked sixty cows that seemed to never get enough attention, and lived for five years in a mobile home. So much for the sweet country way of life I had pictured! I had never worked so hard for so little in my life.

The first year was the most difficult for me. I needed to meet people and get settled into our new hometown. I didn't need any more work. A few dollars to call my own, however, and some time off the farm sounded good.

That's when I heard the schools were hiring bus drivers. It was a part-time job I could fit in with farm work, being gone only a few hours at a time.

When I hired in we had only been here for six months, so I knew where all of the basic stores were but hadn't had time to venture into the countryside much. I didn't know the names of any roads, where they were, or even if they had signs. I was certain that would be part of the bus driver training. Wrong.

Training meant a set of keys, a bus, and a schedule that would hopefully guide us to the school before it started. To top it off, not only had I never driven a school bus before, I couldn't tell you which way was north or south. That should have been a minor detail, cleared up with training. Wrong again.

I Live Next Door to my Neighbor

Training

Let's first clarify what training really means. Training should have been detailed maps and trips with experienced drivers through the country checking out the routes.

Your time driving is more likely to be an early morning wake up call to fill in on a route you've never been on. Where the driver is late before they even answered the phone!

This on-the-job training never includes the routes the new driver spent time on or those that might be slightly remembered in casual conversation. Instead it is finding the corner on which the old gas station burned down about twenty years ago, or going to the old Penrose Farm that hasn't been the Penrose Farm for the past twenty-five years. Training includes directions that have more landmarks that are not there than are there. This is on-the-spot training, finding you misunderstood the route directions, taking someone else's bus by mistake, picking up kids from two different routes, and when you're substituting for another driver forgetting whose route this really is. Training can mean when the new driver gets to the bus garage and finds out that she agreed to drive the route from hell because she didn't know enough to ask which route it was

I Live Next Door to My Neighbor

before she answered, "Sure! No problem. I'll be right in."

If new drivers find that on getting to the bus garage, no one makes eye contact, they are in trouble! Training is something that bus drivers learn as they go along. They don't need notes. They will not soon forget what they went through on those first days of training.

My first time out on a route, my boss, George, handed me the keys and told me to go to the old Wentworth Farm, turn north, and my first students would be there on the west side of the road. Of course, I just smiled and said, "Could you repeat that? You lost me after you handed me the keys."

I have since found that many directions are harder to follow than one might think. {That is, if there was enough information to call them directions in the first place.}

George gives us directions to the first stop and tells us the kids will help us find the rest of the route.

Once I found the right road, but the kids from the first stop weren't riding that particular morning. So I just kept driving until I saw the next set of kids. I turned on my flashing lights, stopped, opened the door, smiled, and the kids just stood there looking at me. I had driven into another school district! The kids knew where they were going and it wasn't with me!

Here is another example of thought-twisting directions. Patti, a fellow bus driver, told me this story. Her boss told her that the first stop was at "my brother's." It seemed simple enough, but when she got to her boss' brother's house she called in to inform the dispatch team that no one was there. Her boss was silent for a moment then shouted, "Not my brother's house! It's My Brother Nursery School!"

Once bus drivers get the training under control, they can

Training

enjoy the kids. They are the best part of driving for me. The young kids are wide-eyed and in awe. The older kids make me wide-eyed. I soon found out that the noise in the bus was more than just whining, complaining, and "drive the bus driver crazy" stuff that gets on one's nerves. These kids were really funny! A lot of the time they thought that they knew what they were saying and would be very serious. This made it even funnier. So, I started to write down what they were saying to share as the "joke of the day" with my mother.

My mom started this sharing shortly after I married and moved into my own home. Any time she heard something funny or really unusual she would take a few minutes to call and say, "Do you want to hear the joke of the day?" We have managed to keep in touch with a quick joke for twenty-five years. Unfortunately, I am one of those people who can't tell a joke because I don't remember all of it. Or I don't remember anything but laughing. So, with each new school year, I found myself wanting to write down my experiences with the children who ride my bus in order to share them with everyone. These are a few of the things the children said that still make me laugh today.

These directions are from children whose homes I had never seen before. The children just know that their instructions will get them home. "Drop me off two houses from Carrie's grandma's house." Or, "I am going to the grandma's with the cookies." And, "I live in the white house with the blue car." Or, "I live next to the old lady with the dog that gets into our garbage." And, of course my very favorite: "I live next door to my neighbor."

With these directions

Children also give "helpful" directions! We live in a small town in Michigan. On the map it's in the center of "the mitten." "Why is this important?" one might ask. Well, I started out as a substitute bus driver and one of my first encounters with a kindergartner involved how to get to this youngster's house. Picture about twenty kids, all age five, getting on a bus after school and discovering that their regular bus driver isn't there. They are smart kids and they know you don't know where they live. I found out that the first lesson was to never confirm what they already knew. Even though I had a list with the children's names and street numbers on it, it wasn't much help. The first boy looked at me face to face and asked, "Do you know where I live?" I must have looked a little lost because before I could answer him I heard a voice behind me say, "Don't worry. I know where everyone lives. Want me to help you?" I gave him a little smile and told him that I'd like that very much. He, in turn, raised his right hand, pointed to the middle of his hand with his left index finger, and proudly said, "We live right here in Michigan." With this kind of help we may never have gotten out of the parking lot!

I Live Next Door to My Neighbor

A little girl was very determined to show me that she knew right where she lived, too. Right off she told me to go down the first "dirty" road and turn "that way," the way she was pointing. "Now keep going until I tell you when to stop," she continued. "Okay. Now do you see that mailbox, that black one right there? See it on that side?" I kept saying, "Yes." "That one right there," she persisted. "Yes, yes," I said. Then she said, "Well, that's not it."

Recently I met Abby, a very smart five year old, when I substituted on the noon route of my fellow bus driver, Karen. We were on a long route and I was having my usual trouble reading the map. I would stop and read, go on, stop, and read. Meanwhile, I noticed Abby sitting in the seat behind me, drawing and shaking her head. When we made eye contact, she told me to turn left at the next corner. I smiled and asked her to show me which one was her left hand. Not even looking at me, she raised the correct one. So I turned and there was my road. During all of this she was drawing. When she got off the bus, she handed me a paper with a lot of lines going everywhere and said, "Next time use this map."

The next time I met up with Abby she was in a more playful mood. I was sitting at a tee in the road and wasn't sure which way to turn. Abby perked up and said, "I will tell you where the next stop is if you will take me home first." I said, "But Abby, you haven't been to school yet." "Yeah, I know," she giggled. "That's the best part."

Argue that one

I had another not-so-daring child. Todd made it right up to my bus and told me that he couldn't get on the bus because his mom told him that he couldn't ride with strangers. Now argue that one with a five year old.

At the beginning of the school year I had a little girl sitting right behind me. Every day I would pull up to the railroad tracks, open the door, look both ways, and go on. After about a week she tapped me on the shoulder and said, "Bus driver, you don't have to stop here anymore. No one ever gets on."

I had a little girl who kept picking her nose. I told her to stop. But, she kept doing it anyway. Finally, I shouted, "Young lady, quit picking your nose, now!" Raising her nose to me, she said, "I almost have it. Can you get it out?"

Not only do kids have trouble with their homes' locations, some have a lot of trouble with who they are. They know key people as Mom and Dad, Grandma, etc. The first night I drove a new route, I noticed a kindergartner was seated in the front

I Live Next Door to My Neighbor

seat. So I asked her what her name was. "Nicole," she whispered. "Nicole what?" I whispered back. "I don't know," she said teary-eyed. "Well, what's your second name?" I asked. "I don't know," she cried. "My mom just calls me Nicole."

At the other extreme, I had one child who told me that his name was Christopher Jonathon Wilson and that he was only going to tell me once. So, I made a point to remember it and said, "Goodnight, Chris", as he got off of the bus. He turned around and said, "It's Christopher Jonathon Wilson, thank you."

One little boy lived a few blocks from the school. I pulled up to his house. Right name on mailbox, right address, his mother jumping up and down in the doorway waving and smiling, and he looked at me and said, "Are you sure?"

Kids can really give a person a lift in life, but not many are as quick-witted as Steven. I was learning a new noon run and this young man named Steven got on the bus. He had a sparkle in his eye just waiting for a chance to turn on his natural abilities. I think I was about to become his favorite target. He took one look at me and said, "Oh great, a rookie! I guess I'll stay home tomorrow and haul manure." Well, at least I knew where riding my bus stood on his list of fun things to do. He got on the bus the next day and I mentioned his chores. He informed me that his tractor broke down and he dropped into a seat behind me, not happy at all. I started out on the route, drove by the first stop, and was looking at the map when Steven decided that I needed help. He told me where the stops were and just before I dropped him off he told me, "I'm going to call your boss,

Argue that one

George, and have him fire you. You would do better feeding the hogs and cows at the stockyard." By this time I could hardly hold back the laughing. Then he took a good look at me and said, "You will have to wear better clothes, but I think they will hire you." Upon returning to the bus garage, George asked me how my run went. I was honest and told him, "I would have quit but I already got fired by Steven. Don't worry, I can still get a job at the stockyards if I was willing to change my wardrobe."

A few years later Steven got on the bus with a Nevada hat on his head. He started pulling yellow tassels out of it and gave them to the kids on the bus. I told him not to ruin such a nice hat. He wore this hat for a long time. One day, when I noticed that he wasn't wearing it anymore, I asked him what happened to it. He looked around sheepishly and said that all of the tassels were gone and that he hid it in his room. From that day on I called him Nevada. He would look around to see if anyone heard me and I'd smile and say, "That's what you get for trying to fire me."

One night I overheard a conversation. Before I had time to comment, the situation cleared up on its own.

Gaby and Jason were having a few words with each other and started calling each other names. Jason pointed at Gaby and told her she was an ugly duckling. Gaby, feeling crushed, looked into my mirror for some support, but Michelle an older girl spoke up first. "You have no right calling her that!" she exclaimed. Jason, now getting a rise from both girls, got an even bigger smile on his face. Then Michelle hit the top of her forehead with her hand and said, "What am I thinking? That ugly

I Live Next Door to My Neighbor

duckling turned into a beautiful swan so you are really telling her is how pretty she is." With that Gabi smiled. I gave a quick look over at Jason, He looked dumb-founded, as he tried to figure out how he had gotten slammed on such an excellent cut. Case closed.

All the little kids sit three to a seat up front. Every day I have to tell them to move over and let the third kid in. Dani, seated behind me hollers, "We already have three to a seat, and we're not moving in, I am putting my foot down on this one!!" Looking into the mirror, I told Dani that I wouldn't be talking to her if she already had three in her seat. Realizing she had made a mistake she replied, "Well, just in case you were, we aren't!!" {A little 60's child running wild?}

One of my fellow drivers, Janis, came into the bus garage and said she had a really good one to share with me today. She had a little boy get on the bus and a few minutes later there was a commotion a few seats back. Janis found out that a very small kitten was on the bus. "Who, might I ask, brought that kitten on this bus?" Janis asked sharply. Several kids pointed to the little boy and said he had just taken it out of his backpack. Janis, not too happy, had to turn the bus around to return the kitten, causing everyone to be a little late for school. When she questioned him on how the kitten got on the bus, he said that it must have followed him up the steps. Janis just gave him that you- know- I- don't- believe- you look. When Janis went to drop off the kids at school he came up to her still proclaiming his innocence, He put his face in hers and said, "Look in this backpack. Do you see any feathers in here?"

Sick kids

I know that as parents we feel very bad when our kids get sick, especially when they are at school and we can't help them. As a bus driver, when I know that kids are sick, I put them up front with me so that I can keep an eye on them. Jenny, a kindergartner, got sick on the bus and her sister sent her to the front to tell me. I took one look and knew that she was going to throw up again. I put the trash box in front of her so that she could get sick in there. But, every time she went to get sick, she would look up to tell me and vomit all over my lap. I was fighting with the seat belt, trying to point her head over the box, while other kids were still trying to squeeze past her to get to their seats. Jenny managed to throw up four times before I could get her off the bus. What a night to have a long route.

―――――――――

Ashley got on the bus one Friday coughing and said, "I can't stand this cold any longer." I gave her a hug and asked her, "How long have you had this cold?" She replied, "Eight minutes."

―――――――――

Baby sitter

This brings us to the interesting job of babysitting, or figuring out after-school schedules. Most families have both parents working and things are timed around their jobs. So, on Tuesday and Thursday, Amy would get off at the sitter's. Friday she got off at her grandma's. Every other Monday she had dance lessons, and Wednesday she went home, unless otherwise informed! Whew!

I had one little girl who I knew was supposed to get off the bus at her sitter's house. I arrived there, opened the bus door, and she said, "I don't go here anymore." I asked, "Since when?" "Since she raised her prices. I now go to the sitter's with the white house and the blue car." White and blue must be the standard colors.

I picked up children at a sitter's house that always had a different number of children getting on the bus each day. One day, I went all the way to the school, let the kids off, and two kids stayed on the bus. So, I asked them, "What's wrong?" They responded, "We're waiting to go back to Mrs. Blystone's house.

I Live Next Door to My Neighbor

We just wanted to ride a school bus."

Sometimes parents try to get as much done as possible while the kids are in school, and they don't always get back home in time to meet the bus. One afternoon I dropped Joey off at his house, and went down the road to turn the bus around. Upon heading back, I noticed a set of feet slipping through the living room window. So I stopped, beeped the horn, and out came Joey. "Joey, isn't there anyone home?" I asked. "Sure! I'm home," he responded, smiling. "I know that. How about your mom or dad?" "Nope. Why?" he asked. Now, I could tell this was bothering me more than him. "Well, what are you going to do until they get home?" I questioned. With a big grin he said, "I am going to take the boat out and go fishing." Needless to say, WE waited for his mom.

Then there are the kids who get on the bus with so many notes pinned on them they look like walking memo boards—notes for teachers sitters, bus drivers etc.—Sarah was so tired of keeping track of all her notes that when I asked which one was mine, she looked at me and said, "Just pick one."

Another time, I went to drop off a child at a sitter's house and found that no one was home. I sat there for a few minutes. Thinking out loud, I said, "Now where do I take you?" The little girl, perking right up, responded, "If you have peanut butter and jelly at your house, I'll go with you."

Beware of kids bearing gifts

It was Christmas and the kids gave their teachers and bus drivers presents. I was subbing for Lois. She was receiving quite a few gifts, so I assured the kids that she would get them. One girl handed me a bag of cookies and peanuts that happened to look like someone had sat on them. She smiled and said that they were just for me. "Thank you. Did you help your mother make these?" I asked. "Oh, no," she said "I found them back there on the floor under the seat."

I received a small inexpensive gift from Jasmine, one of my four year olds. When she gave it to me I made an extra special fuss over it. "It's just what I wanted. How did you know?" "I didn't," she said. "It was the only thing the man in the store said I had enough money for."

I was talking to Cassie, one of my second graders, one day. She was telling me how much she liked to collect stickers. I told her my favorite things to collect are anything to do with angels. I showed her my small collection of angel stickers on the bus and told her I had a lot of other angel things at home.

I Live Next Door to My Neighbor

Several weeks later it was Christmas-time and a very excited Cassie came to the bus to give me a gift. Opening it, I found a beautiful book on angels. Before I got very far browsing through the book, she informed me, "Don't forget to get it back to the library in two weeks."

One of the newer drivers, Sharon, had been watching us open gifts in the bus garage. She reached in her pocket and pulled out a gift. She said a boy on her bus had given it to her and he was so excited that he wanted her to open it right away. She did and inside the package were two AA batteries. She smiled at the boy and said, "Thank you so much." Perking right up, he said, "All you have to do is recharge them."

I have received many homemade cards over the years. The one I received from Nicole and Jessica was among my favorites. The front of the card, written in wobbly cursive handwriting, said, "To a wonderful bus driver" and the inside read, "You've been making good time. Thank you."

Another card had a picture of a bus and all kinds of kids in each window on the front. Inside it said, "You are the greatest driver ever. I can't hear a word you say. Love, Raquel."

"To the super best driver ever," Kaelynn wrote on the inside of her card. She continued, "If you didn't pick up kids, this would be a nice bus."

One card read, "To my favorite driver," on the outside. On

Beware of kids bearing gifts

the inside it said, "Please, hurry. I need a bathroom!"

"Merry Christmas to my favorite bus driver," said a card that I received several Christmases ago. "Sorry, Mom gave your present to the garbage men" was the heart-warming sentiment on the inside.

No eating on bus until further notice

Some kids like to share things and Joe liked to bring me something from his lunch. I think it started as a whole piece. But he would nibble on it! By the time he got to the bus he would hand me a small, sticky, half-melted piece of whatever it was, always with a big grin from ear to ear.

I'd like to compliment parents on the creative lunches they fix their kids. I'd also like to inform them that 50 percent of the lunches never make it to the lunchroom. Chad, just one of the many children who enjoy the lunches lovingly packed by his parents, got on the bus one morning and first thing he did was to go to his seat and open his lunch pail. There was no reason to look at him to know what he was doing. The smell of bologna, mayonnaise, bananas, and some form of chocolate drifted to the front of the bus. "Chad, get out of your lunch," I said. "Bus driver, I'm just looking," he commented. "Look at noon", was my reply. And so this started our day.

Later that day on the bus Chad returned to finish his lunch on the bus trip home. He tore off all of his bread crusts and threw them into the trash. He then retrieved a strawberry

I Live Next Door to My Neighbor

banana yogurt, which had gotten a bit runny after six hours. When he pulled it out to eat on the bus, thinking that it was going to be really good stuff, I informed him that he could wait until he got home or he could throw it out right now. That's one mess I was not going to clean up. By that time the kids were talking to me about their teachers and what they did in school that day. In addition, Trista just had to show me her finger paintings. While I was trying to run through ten pages of half-dry sticky pictures, Chad decided to throw out his yogurt. I looked up and found him pouring it out of the carton, into the garbage. All I would like to say is, "Yes, the garbage tipped over on the way home, creating the mess that I hadn't wanted to clean up."

"Tim, I understand that you were eating on the bus today. Is this true?" I asked."No," Tim announced with truth on his side, "I didn't chew, I only swallowed!"

I had been having a lot of trouble with the younger kids throwing papers, candy wrappers, etc. on the floor of the bus. Every morning I had to sweep up their mess. After a few days, I decided to have a talk with them. "From now on," I said, "You kids will have some new jobs on this bus." Before I could get another word out Andrew spoke up and said, "So when are you going to start taking interviews?"

"Due to the mess on the floor of my bus," I informed the kids, there will be no more eating on the bus until further notice." Within about three minutes of my announcement one of

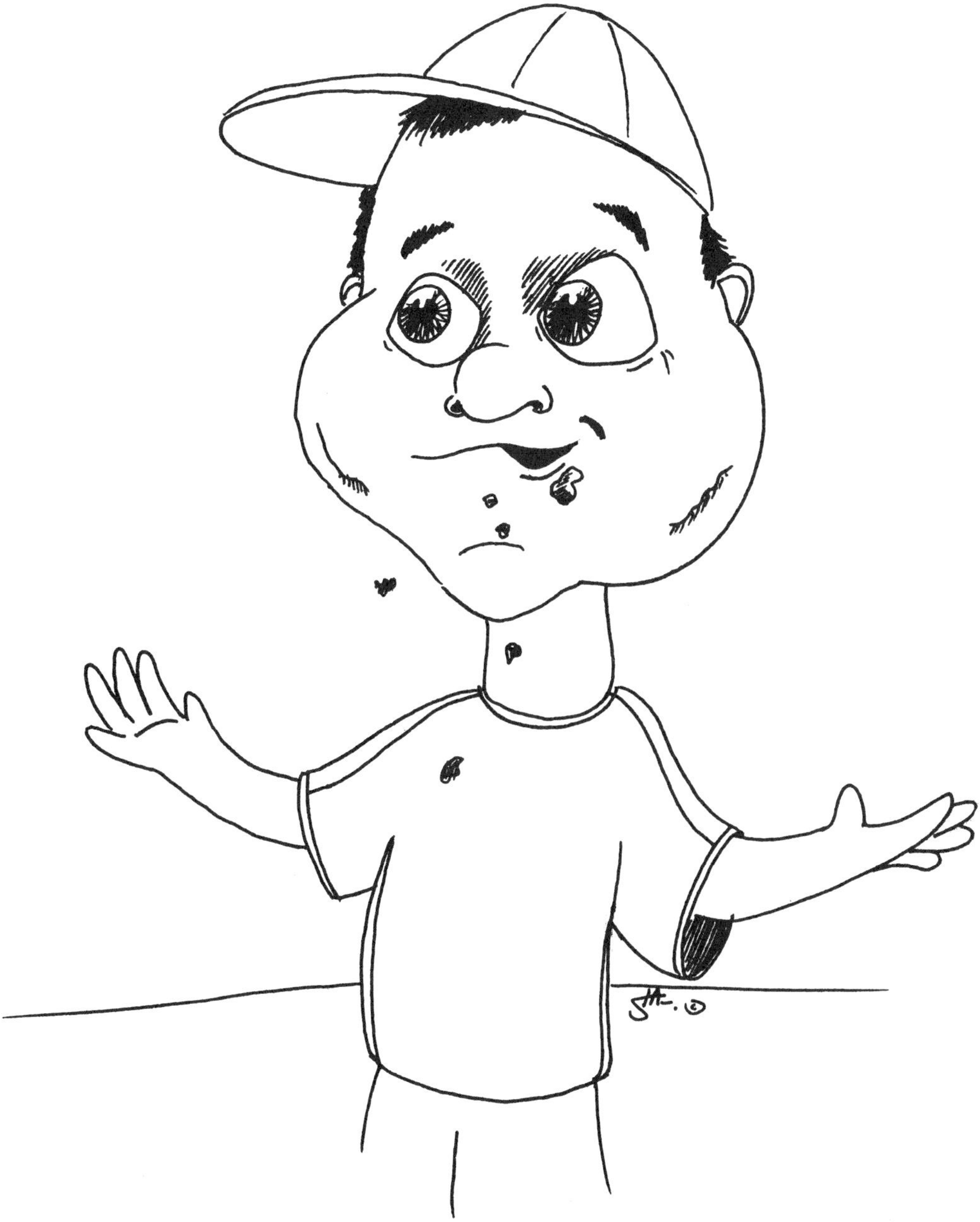

I Live Next Door to My Neighbor

my first graders asked, "Have you changed your mind yet? I still have stuff to eat."

Upon my announcement of "no eating on the bus," children moaned, grumbled, rolled their eyes, and started a barrage of questions:

1. "Is a sucker considered food?"
2. "Does gum count?"
3. "Does it count if you already started to eat something?"
4. "I have never dropped anything on the floor, was that 'no eating' meant for me too?"
5. "Is 'until further notice' just for today?"
6. "Can't we start tomorrow? I am starving!"
7. "I never throw anything on the floor. I put it in the little hole in the back of the seat!"
8. "Does it count if you are more than halfway done?"
9. "Can I swallow this or should I spit it out?"
10. "If we promise never, never, ever to make a mess again, will you let us eat right now?"

Smiling, one of my first graders got on the bus with a Tupperware bowl full of cookies to take to her class. When we got to school, she came up to me looking in the now empty bowl and said, "I need a ride back home."

One of my first graders who was getting off the bus had a mouth full of food. Before I had a chance to say anything, Kyle spoke around the food, "I didn't eat this. I am just getting it ready to."

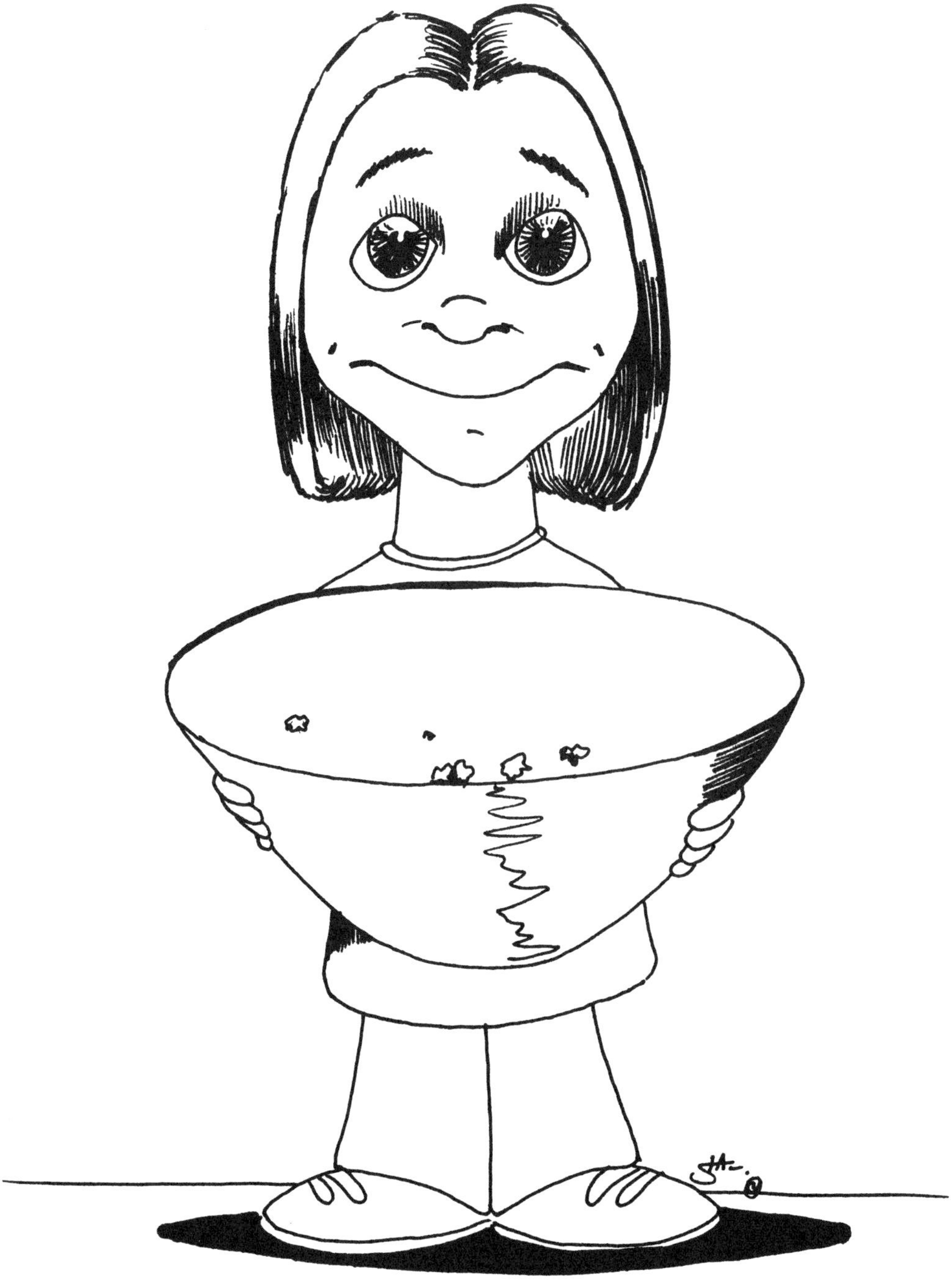

I Live Next Door to My Neighbor

Matthew is another young farmer on my bus. As his dad waited by my bus to pick him up after school one day, he shared this cute story with me.

Matt and his dad, Reggie, had gone to the stockyards in another state the previous week to work. Reggie couldn't get away to buy Matt any lunch, so he told the lady at the lunch counter to let him charge what he would like to eat. By the end of the day Reggie went into pay up and he had a bill for about forty-eight dollars! Everything Matt had ordered was a la cart, and he had bought a few candy bars and things to enjoy later. Well, Reggie had learned his lesson. The next day they made a stop at the grocery store to pick up some bologna and bread. Satisfied that he covered his bases, Reggie went back to work. At lunchtime Reggie went back to the truck all ready for his lunch. There he found Matt finishing a bologna sandwich that he had made with every slice of meat on it. His dad still didn't get any lunch!

One of the last field trips I went on was with four year-olds. They have to be watched very carefully so you usually get a chaperon for every two to three kids. On this trip we went to a Mexican restaurant fifteen miles away from the school. There are plenty of songs to sing in that short of a time.

Getting to the restaurant the owner had all the tables set up with drinks, chips, salsa, guacamole dip, crayons, and paper. The children found seats immediately and started their one-of-a-kind pictures. All was going well until the owner wanted to give the kids a tour of the kitchen. Half of the kids were to stay with the fun stuff on the tables and the rest were to go to the kitchen. Moaning and completely unhappy, they went in, leaving the lucky ones to the extra chips. The kitchen was narrow so

No eating on the bus until further notice

there was a line of kids being told, "Hot!" "Don't touch!" "Keep moving!" By the time they got up to the owner, he was talking about deep fryers, and all the hard to pronounce things he made in there. The children, being very small, could not see much more than the legs and underside of the work surface. Upon returning to the table one four year old asked the other, "Did ya see anything?" He quickly replied, "Nope."

Hope brought a big red apple up to the front of the bus, and asked if I would like to eat it. I told her, "No, thank you". Then, she asked if I would hold it so she could get a Kleenex. I said, "Sure." To my surprise, the apple was already half eaten!

Two first graders were sitting in the front seat. Gaby had a small pudding left over from lunch, but no spoon. Heather had a sucker. Gaby said, "I don't have any thing to eat my pudding with." Heather, being helpful, dunked her sucker in the pudding and said, "Well, all you need is one of these." Next thing I knew Gaby was eating her pudding with her index finger. When she finished she showed me how clean her index finger was compared to her other ones. Mother would be so proud!

The other day it was a younger girl's birthday and she brought cupcakes to school. Smiling, she told me that her mom had sent one for me, too. When we arrived at school she came up to me with the cupcake—licked clean of all of the frosting—in her hand. I looked up at her and saw some of my frosting still on her smiling face. Without any hesitation, she handed me my cupcake. She would share her cake, but the frosting was just too tempting.

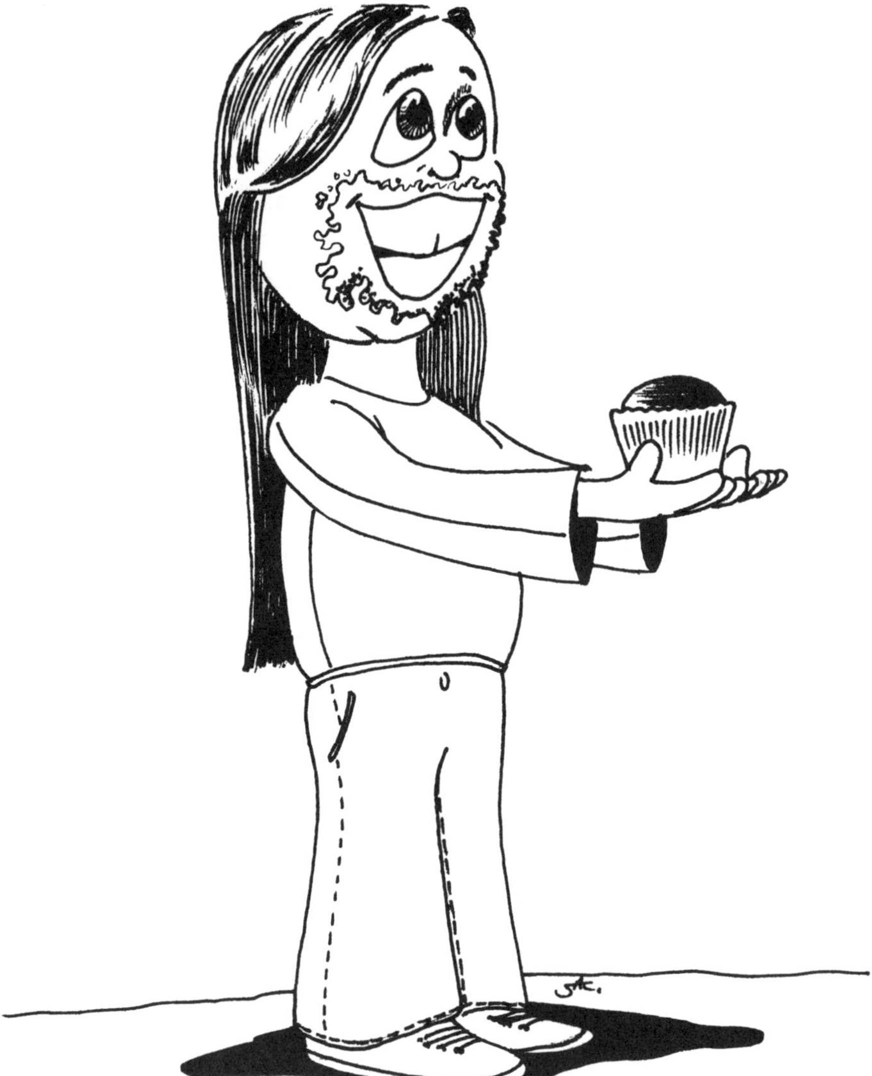

Missing teeth

The younger children lose their teeth at about five years old. Tracy was sitting on the seat behind me looking into the mirror, counting her teeth. She told me that as soon as her first tooth came out, the tooth fairy was going to give her two big "bird nickels" and a dollar. It took some thought on my part, but I figured out that "bird nickels" are quarters.

Tess had a loose tooth and on the way to the bus she fell down and it came out. She ran up to me and said that she wanted me to put it back in! I looked at her, then at the tooth, and said, "I'm sorry, but you can't put it back in there once it comes out." Opening her mouth real wide, she said, "Yes, you can. I can see the hole it belongs in."

Liz had about four or five teeth missing in the front. She informed me that her boyfriend was going to dump her if she lost one more tooth. Looking into my mirror, turning her smiling face from side to side, she said, "But, I rather like my new look."

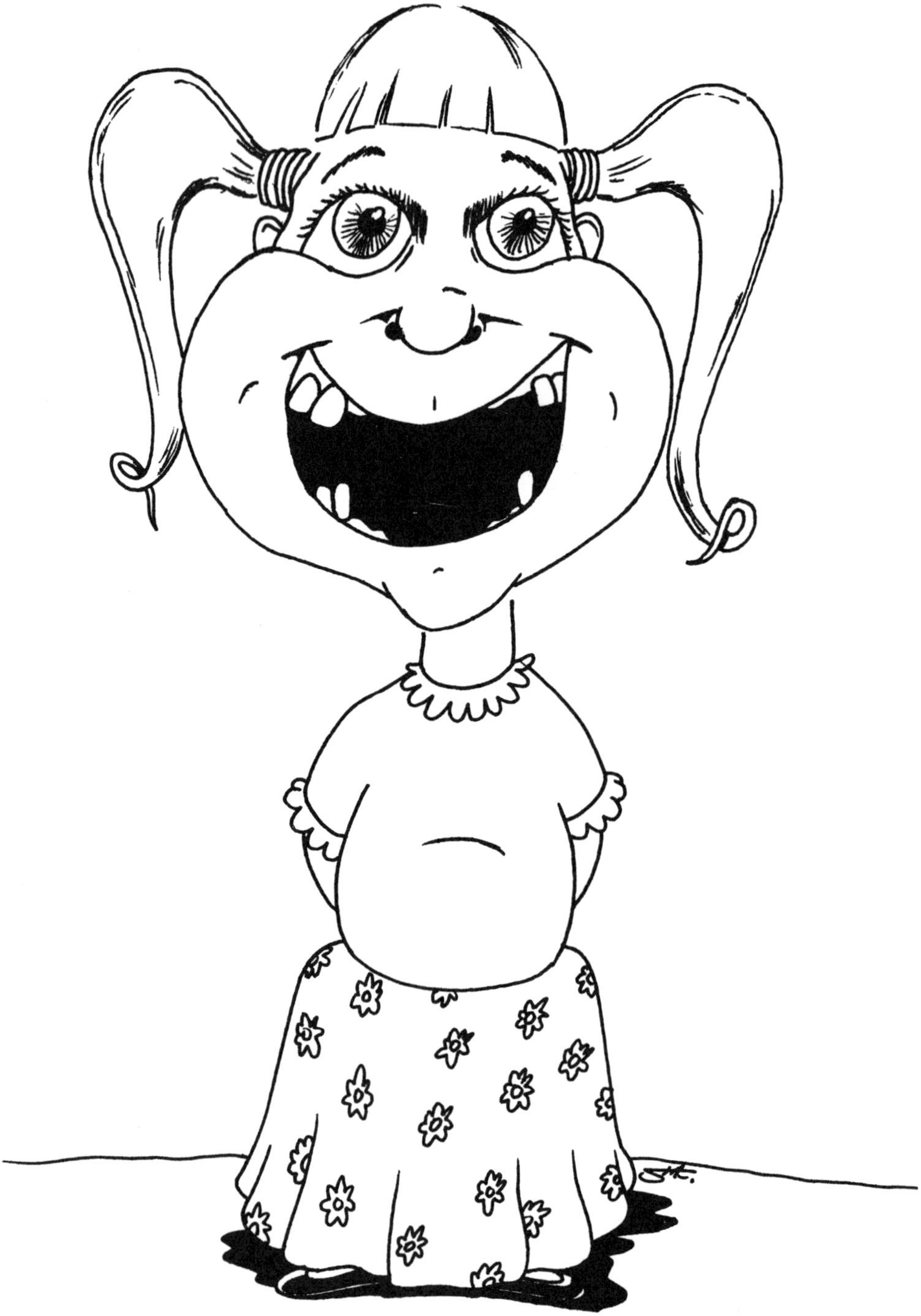

Missing teeth

Carrie's problem was that she didn't have a place to keep her tooth after it came out. So I gave her a Kleenex to wipe her mouth, and one to wrap the tooth in. By the time we got to her house she was in tears. She decided to put the tooth in a safe place and accidentally swallowed it!

Leave this kind of logic to come from a seven-year-old boy. This little boy told me that his grandfather could take his teeth out all at one time and that he wanted teeth just like that. "What on earth for?" I asked. He looked at me like it made all of the sense in the world. "Well, then I could take them out and have my mom brush them!" he exclaimed.

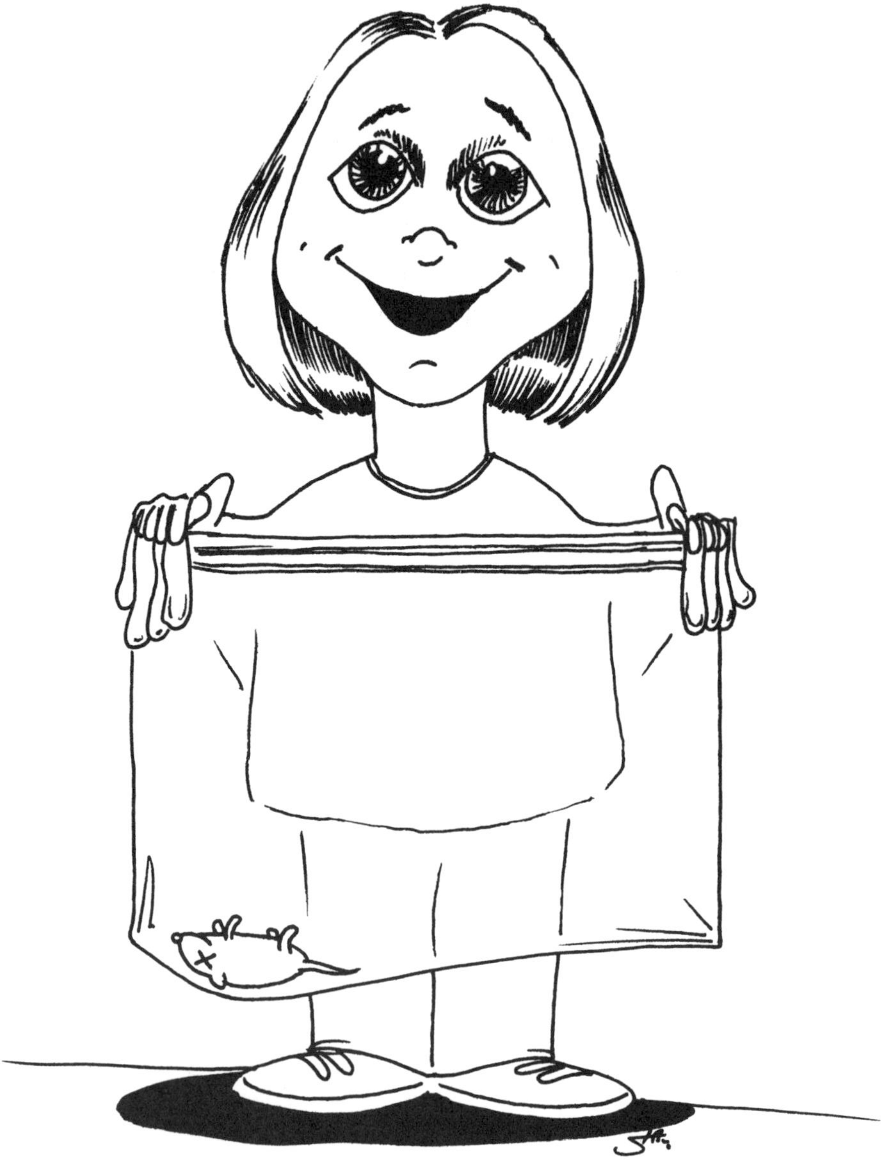

Two thousand crawling things

Children have about two thousand different crawling, jumping, slithering, smelly, "I-don't-know-where-you-got-it-from," things that they want to bring on the bus. According to them, they are either pets or science projects. My buddy, Carrie, got on the bus the other day wearing latex gloves and was carrying something in a baggie. I told her that whatever it was I didn't want it out of that bag. My curiosity was aroused, however, and I asked her what she had. "Oh, it's something I found and I want the teacher to tell me what it is," she said. So I asked her, "What do you think it is?" Taking another look in her bag, she responded, "Well, I am pretty sure that it's the dead mouse my dad threw out of the kitchen a week ago."

We drove by an opossum lying on the side of the road. Timmy felt bad that it was dead. I started to tell him how opossums will play dead when they are frightened or in danger. This seemed to make him feel better and I changed the subject. Three days later as he looked out the window, he tapped me on the shoulder and said, "I am glad I am not a opossum. I couldn't play dead that long!"

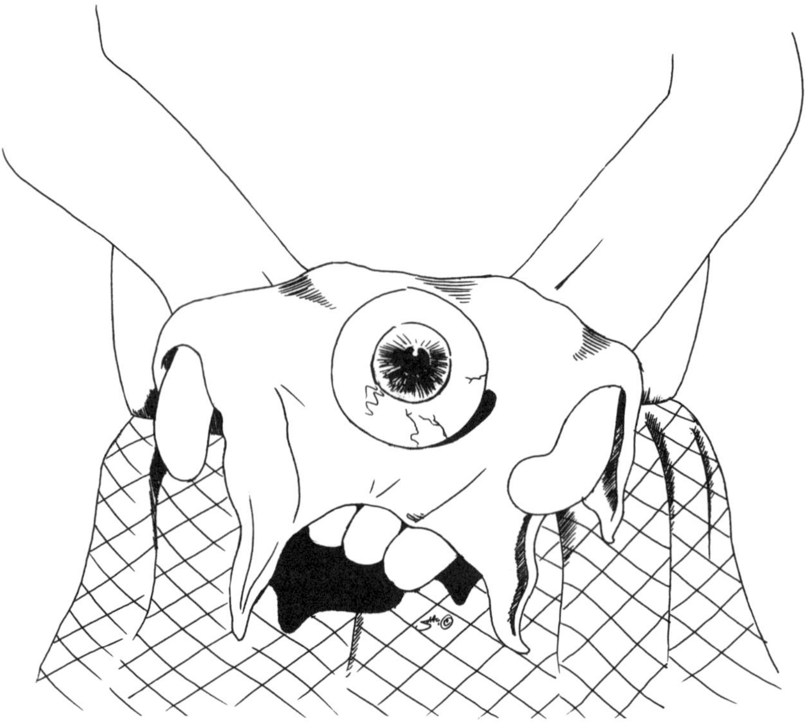

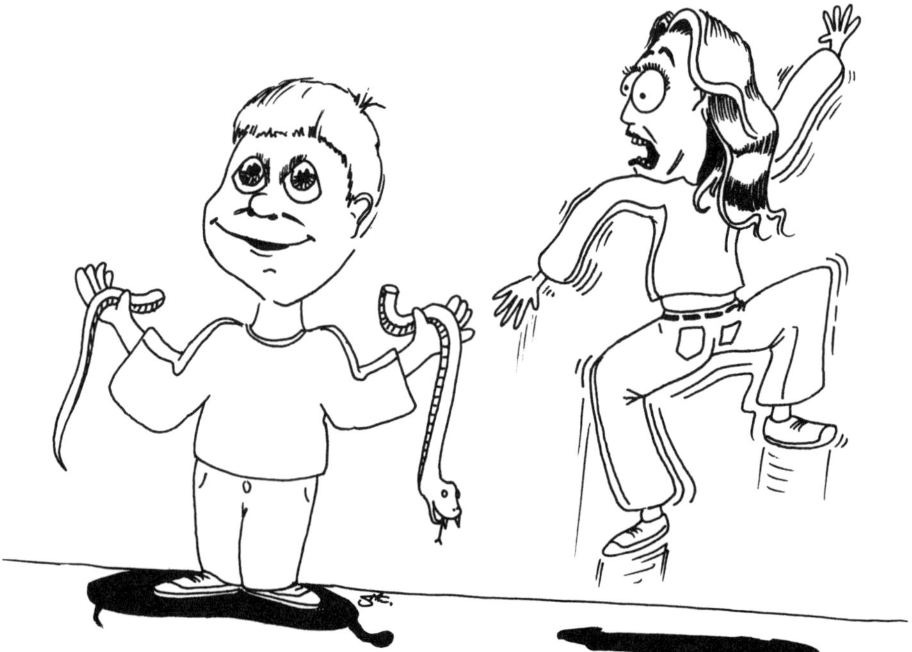

Two thousand crawling things

Carrie likes to sit up front with me. In the morning she is one of the first kids on the bus. We talk about all kinds of things. Today was quite the topper as she pointed out the window at a bunch of chickens and asked, "Do you know what those are?" "Well, my guess would be chickens," I replied. Rolling her eyes, she said, "Heavens no! Those are Canadian ostriches." Holding back from laughing, I asked her if she was sure. "I am positive," she said. "All the Amish have those kind."

Carrie also introduced me to snow snakes. Blowing snow dancing across the road reminds her of slithering snakes.

The other day Michelle got on the bus with something wrapped in a paper towel. I just thought that it was part of her lunch or something. Then I heard one of the kids say, "You're going to get in trouble for taking that out of school." Michelle said, "I plan on bringing it back tomorrow." So I stepped in to see what she had. It was a lamb's eyeball that they were going to dissect in class the next day.

I was talking to the other drivers about things that kids bring on the bus and we got on the subject of snakes. Mary, who is deathly afraid of snakes, told her kids that none of them had better even think about bringing one on her bus. The seed had been planted. Later that night, a boy brought up a rubber snake that was broken for her to fix. Nobody ever knew that Mary could move so fast.

Another driver I knew had a similar thing happen, only that time it was a real snake that had been dropped on the floor.

I Live Next Door to My Neighbor

Trying to maintain a calm and organized group, she told all the kids in a very loud, shaky voice to get back into their seats. "Everything is under control!" she exclaimed. On shouting it for the third time, she noticed someone tugging on her pant leg. Looking up at her, the child said, "I would sit down if you would get your feet off my seat."

I was very happy when our school finally put radios on all of the buses. Breaking down and having to get off the bus to use the phone is quite hard, especially if a person is afraid of dogs like I am. I can have an anxiety attack with one barking Chihuahua. It is bad when a farmer has a small dog, but some have no less then a herd of them! I have shut kids' coats in the door, trying to close it before Fido can get on the bus, too. Let's face it. If that dog wants that kid to stay home and play, I'm willing to leave him there.

One morning my greatest fear was realized. Fido got on the bus! I know that I should have made the dog leave, but I was trying to get my breathing back under control. He followed Tommy to his seat, jumped up, and sat beside him. I told Tommy that the dog would have to leave, but I could not bear the thought of it walking past me again. So we backed into his driveway and I had him take his dog out the back door of the bus, run around to the front door, and get back on. Tommy jumped on the bus and said, "That was so cool! Can we do it again tomorrow?"

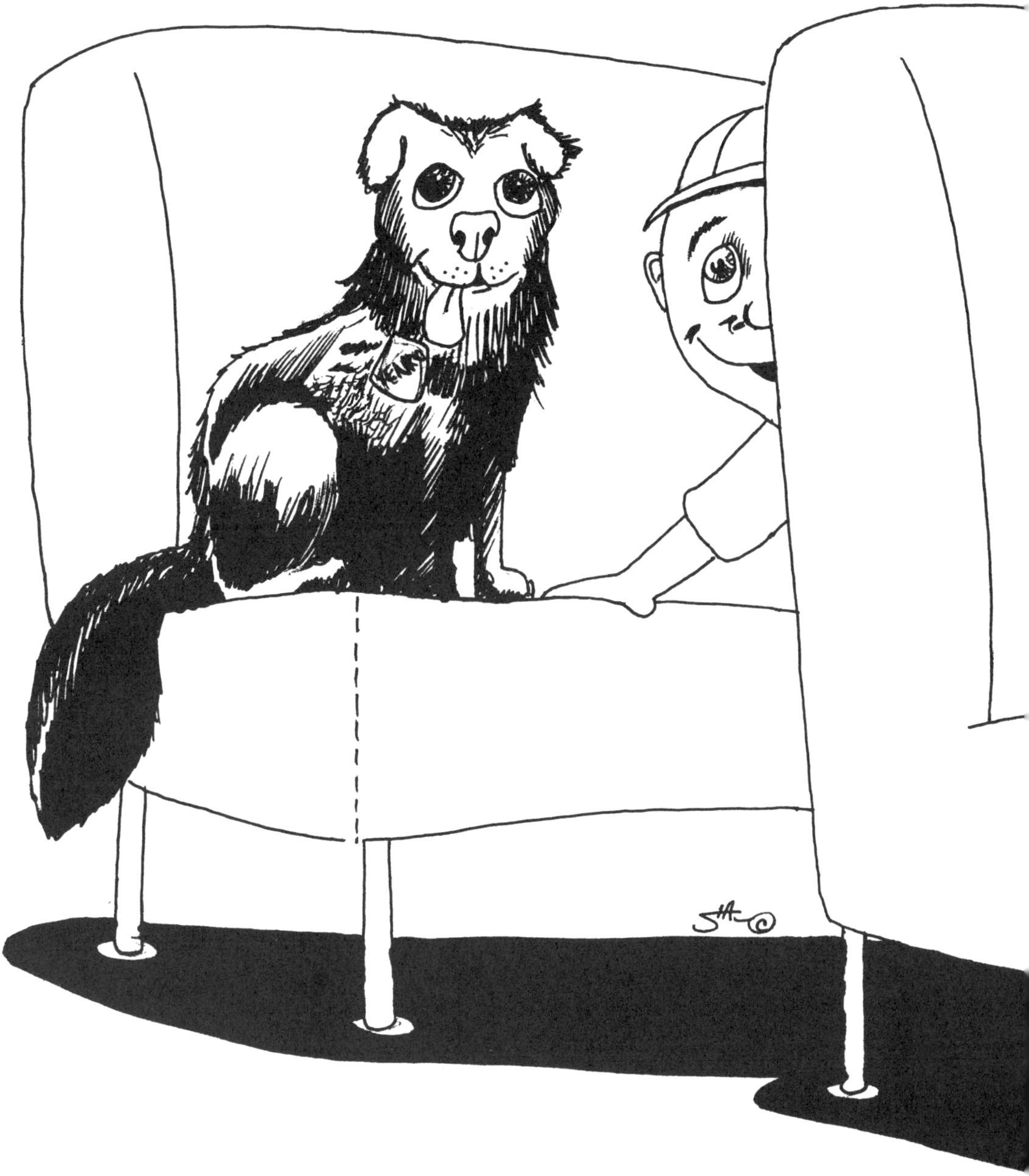

When you gotta go

Here it is September again and the first days of school are just beginning.

I had forgotten that the children have to give a fashion show as they get on the bus. They each have to let me check out their new outfits and the shoes that light up every time they take a step. The new haircuts and big smiles make me realize how much I had missed them. "It's great to be back." I think. Then reality strikes: The kids are now a year older and they have a new pecking order to establish before the first hellos can be made. The seniors have the very last seats, which is no problem because there are only two of them this year. Ah, but there is twenty new high school students all wanting to sit in the next two seats.

Then, two of the third graders had a fight during the summer and refused to sit on the same bus let lone two seats apart.

Glancing into my mirror, I noticed Heather, a first grader, with her face in the breeze of the window and her shirt off. "Heather," I stammered. " Please, put your shirt on immediately!" "Oh, Deb," she smiled. "It is just like sitting in front of my fan." Upon glancing into the mirror again, I saw that she had

I Live Next Door to My Neighbor

taken her shirt, and wrapped it under her arms, and tied it in the back. "How does this look?" she inquired. "Is that the way your mother dressed you this morning?" I asked her. "No, but it's going to be hot today." "Fine," I said. "Put your shirt on now and let your teacher handle your wardrobe changes."

There was also a little three year old who was unable to speak very clearly. As we went down the road, I mistook his loud whooping for enjoying his bus ride, until I heard one word very clearly: "Pee!" I shot a glance into my mirror and Chelsea, a third grader, was looking back at me. Nodding her head up and down, she said, "Deb, this kid has his pants pulled down and I think he is serious!" Waiting was not on this child's mind. I quickly pulled my bus over and got our littlest child off the bus and pointed in the right direction. That's when I felt this warm feeling come over my leg and foot. He had turned, looked up at me with this big gracious grin, and was peeing on my leg. All I could think of at that moment was that there were only 179 more days left!"

There have been a few times that I have had mechanical breakdowns with the bus. Parents who have had car trouble know how quick their kids' moods can change. Now, add about a dozen more kids and you'll know where I am coming from. One day, we broke down about ten miles out of town. I made a phone call and was told that help would be there soon. The directions got misplaced, however, and we ended up waiting for over an hour. We were playing word games when one boy mentioned "Mom." Three kids started crying, Tommy said he was hungry, two kids were fighting over a match-box car, and one kid was telling me for the hundredth time that he had to go to the bathroom! I didn't know how much longer it was going to be. So,

SCHOOL BUS

first things first, I started looking for a place for Donny to go to the bathroom. I took him off of the bus, but he wouldn't go until I promised him that no one could see him. I got back on and moved all of the kids to the opposite side of the bus. I got back out, turned my back on Donny, looked up to the bus, and saw that every window had a nose pressed on it. That put a new meaning to "no peeking"!

One afternoon I had a four-year-old child who seemed a little upset about riding the bus. He couldn't speak clearly, so I had trouble understanding him. Thinking that he was upset about the ride home, I tried to comfort him by talking. Finally, we made it to his house where his smiling mother was waiting by the driveway. Pulling up to the drive, I opened the door to tell his mom how well her little trooper had done. The child stepped off of the bus, and his mother and I continued chatting. After our conversation we both looked at him and saw that he had pulled the front of his pants down and was relieving himself on the side of the bus. His eyes were closed and he wore a very large smile. Just in the nick of time!

I had a young man who needed to go to the bathroom soon after we left the school, but felt he could make it home. With some doubt, I continued the route. Within fifteen minutes he started to ask how much longer until we reached his house. Another ten minutes passed and he was very uncomfortable. Ten minutes later, he was ready to bust. Crying now, he begged me to let him out to go the bathroom. So, I stopped the bus in a driveway and let him out with the suggestion of going behind a small tree near the driveway. When I did my routine check of

When you gotta go

my mirrors, I found him standing by the bus in such a spot that he showed up in four of my seven mirrors! So much for privacy!

Tammy, a three-year-old preschooler, would walk to the bus with her sister. During the winter she had to wear a snowsuit and hat. She couldn't bend her arms and walked stiff-legged. One chilly morning as she managed to get to the steps, I looked down and all I saw were two little blue eyes peering out of the double-wrapped scarf around her face. From this bundled up angel I heard a little voice. "I gotta pee." It must go with the suit.

Almost have it right

Mary Margaret, a second grader who went to the Catholic school, came to the bus pretty excited one afternoon. I asked her what was up and she said, "I learned about the lady with the fruit today." I asked, "What lady with fruit?" She said, "You know the prayer, Hail Mary full of grapes."

———————

I had a four year old who rode my bus. One afternoon Johnny decided to sing. He only knew one line of the song and repeated it over and over again. He began singing, "Jesus is the son of God." After a short time he was singing "Jesus lies in the sun on the sod... Amen."

———————

Al was repeating the Pledge of Allegiance to me. He had learned it that day in school. I noticed that he had a couple of words wrong. He proudly recited, "I pledge allegiance to the flag of the United States of America and for Richard Sands..."

———————

Denny and I had a conversation about drugs and what they could do to you. He was quite young and I was trying to keep it

I Live Next Door to My Neighbor

simple. "If you use drugs, you could damage your brain so badly that you could end up a vegetable," I explained to him. Several days later he was talking to one of his friends on the bus and said, "If you use drugs, you can turn into a carrot."

At the beginning of the school year, on the first day that our four year olds rode the bus, I was waiting for them after school. I heard this loud shrill and when I looked out of the bus door there stood Heather with her hands on her head screaming, "Ms. Frizzle, Ms. Frizzle, you brought the magic school bus with you!" Jumping up and down clapping her hands she shouted, "Where are you taking me today?" I had no idea that Ms. Frizzle was an eccentric teacher on a TV show about a magic school bus or that she took students on adventures all over the universe. For two weeks, every time she came to the bus, Heather screamed and went through her entire dance!

Heather, a kindergartner, was on the bus sitting with her four-year-old brother. They had been arguing when Heather finally said, "Johnny, if you don't leave me alone, I am going to run away and join the Chinese!"

Heather, one of my first graders, confided in me that her youngest sibling was a half sister. Knowing the family, I asked why she thought that. "Well, first Mom said my sister was half my size, then she told me she was half my age," Heather, logically explained. "So that makes her my half sister." "But of course." I answered.

I was talking to the kids as they got on the bus for the ride

Almost have it right

home. As I asked them what grade they were in this year, several kids answered by showing me one finger and two had showed me two fingers. Then this little kindergartner looked at his hands and then at me saying, " I don't have a number."

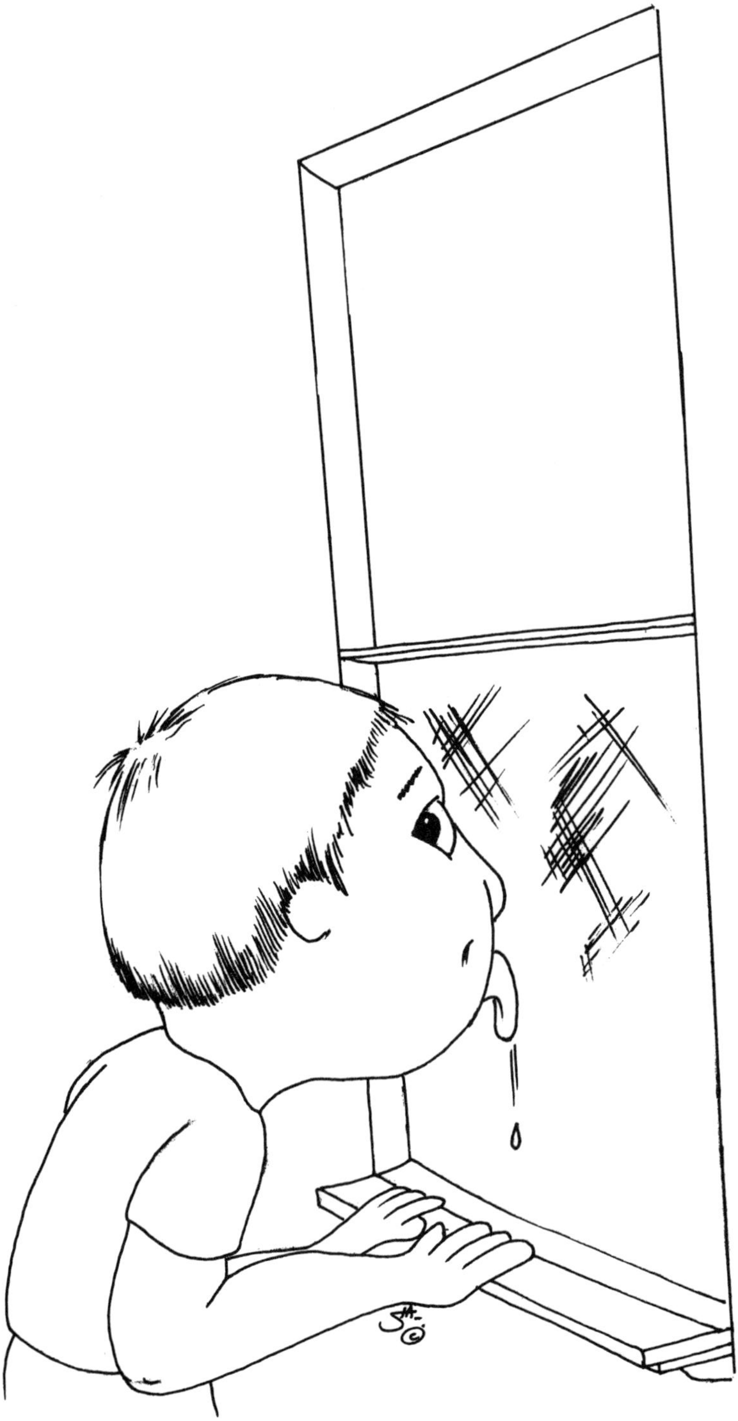

You'll have that

Another time, I went on a field trip with a group of four year olds. Jim, another driver, referred to them as "window lickers." I thought that was funny. A few days later I found one of my kids licking the frost from the inside of the windows. "Please, don't lick that window," I said. He responded, "I'm just getting a drink."

Some of the best artwork is done on the frosted windows. We get all sizes of handprints and animal paw prints. The little ones have to see if their tongues will stick to the metal. Kids scrape the frost off with their nails, fling it at their neighbors, and leave abstract designs on the windows. They also practice spelling all of the words that they have ever heard. Finally, they torment the person seated two seats away with the name of his or her newest love written on the window in large letters with hearts and kisses randomly placed all around. Cupid's art work gets done with such flair sometimes.

Richard has always been a handful on or off the bus. His seat is right behind me. Once when I got on the bus I caught Richard

I Live Next Door to My Neighbor

spitting on the boy behind him. "Richard, just what do you think you're doing?" I snapped. "I spit on him cuz he spit on me first," he replied. "Next time you better let me handle it," I told him. Wide-eyed, Richard looked right at me and said, "Why? Are you gonna spit on him, too?"

Perry got on the bus and accidentally called me Mom. He laughed and said, "Did you hear me? I just called you Mom!" "Yes, I heard you," I replied. Still laughing, he said, "I can't believe I called you Mom! You don't even smell like her!"

Michelle was having a little trouble sitting still on the bus. I had to correct her several times a day, every day. One morning she gave me a piece of candy. Hoping this would be the turning point for us, I took the candy and thanked her. That night she came back to the bus and asked where her candy was. Looking a little stunned, I said, "I thought that it was for me." "Well," she said, "how do you like being in trouble for no reason?"

Maybe T.J. watched too many soap operas. One morning he rode the bus. T.J. didn't ride the bus often and was paying special attention to all of the noise around him. Kids were fighting, arguing, and name-calling and he just stared at them. Then, looking up at me, he said, "It's like, 'As the Bus Turns.'"

Timmy was a new student on my route who never rode a bus before. Within a few weeks he had a field trip and I happened to be the driver. He was quite excited. Then he started looking around and said, "Do you have a house or do you live in this bus?"

You'll have that

Ben was so excited to get home from school that he ran across the lawn, fell down, and dropped his eyeglasses. Megan, another student, said, "Hey! He didn't go back and pick them up." I asked if she was positive. She couldn't tell for sure. Several days later Ben's mom called looking for his glasses. I blurted out, "I sure hope you haven't mowed the lawn yet!"

There was a girl on the bus who loved to tease and keep everyone stirred up. She didn't like it, however, if someone teased her back. One day, she stormed up to the front of the bus and said, "Now don't tell me you didn't hear him that time." I looked at her and replied, "I am sorry, but I really didn't hear him." Fuming, she said, "Maybe we need to hide a tape recorder back there so you can catch what they are saying." Before I could answer though, she added, "Maybe we should think about this some more."

I take care of my little niece on Tuesdays, so she rides with me on my route. On the way to the bus, she dropped her Mother's Day plant twice. When she finally made it, she asked if I would hold on to it for her so that it wouldn't get ruined. I put it on the ledge by my window. Like usual, Gaby fell asleep half-way around the route. Going down a very bumpy road, my side window opened and out swoosh went Gaby's gift! I could not believe that I hadn't seen that one coming. It was like in slow motion. I stopped the bus and went back to get the card and to see if I could save any of the plant. Nope. It disintegrated on contact. Walking back, I looked up to see Gaby waiting at the top of the steps. "I am so sorry, Gaby," I moaned. "Oh, that's okay, Aunt Debbie," she said. "We have enough flowers to water at home."

I Live Next Door to My Neighbor

Mike, a new kindergartner, arrived at the bus with his bib overalls on and a pencil in his top pocket. Grinning, he informed that me he got to go to school like his older brothers. At the end of the day, Mike got on the bus a lot less enthused. He told me that they have too much work on the farm for him to do to be coming back the next day. Throwing his hands in the air, he announced, "They don't get anything done in there!"

Lester

I always thought that I had pretty good communication with the kids on my buses. Some kids just have a good line and you never forget them. Lester was one of those kids. He could be a lot of trouble and it was getting to the point where I would get a headache just watching him head for the bus. When he was just a kindergartner, I knew that he would ride every day until he graduated. Nothing worked to keep him in his seat or to leave the other kids alone. So I came up with the idea of a starboard. Every time Lester was good on the bus I gave him a gold star to put on his poster. One night this was not working, so I told him to behave and we would do something special when he got off the bus. When we arrived at his house, I opened the door for him and told him to scream as loud as he could. He did and was so good at it that his mother came out to see what was going on. I think she wondered if I'd finally cracked and had her son by the throat. Soon the school invested in a seat belt for Lester and I kept praying that he might move.

Lester liked to make animal noises. He once howled like a coyote for three weeks. As Lester was making monkey noises

I Live Next Door to My Neighbor

one morning, I turned around to find him hanging upside down by his knees over the seat. I am not the only one who had nightmares over this kid. I think his mom did, too. Lester was in a generous mood one day. When he got off the bus, some kids said that he had given them money and asked if they could keep it. I asked, "How much was it?" They started handing me ten and twenty dollar bills. Catching up with him, we found out that he taken his mom's money she had set aside to pay bills, and had about $150 on him.

Lester and his brother were not out at the bus stop. Just as I was ready to leave, Lester ran out. He jumped on the bus and asked me to wait for his brother. I waited several minutes and asked if he was sure John was coming. Lester replied, "Oh yes, I woke him up on my way out the door."

Lester was telling me about the twister-volcano he had learned about that day. I asked, "Well, which one was it?" Lester said, "You know the one. You go out in the hallway, put your head between your legs, and wait until the bell rings."

One morning a little girl brought some chocolate on the bus and shared it with Lester and her girlfriend. The two girls decided that they didn't like it and gave the rest to Lester who very happily ate it all. Several days later I asked his brother why Lester hadn't been riding. He informed me that what Lester had eaten wasn't chocolate but a box of Ex-Lax.

School pictures

Missing teeth, hair out of place, crooked smiles and mismatched colors—these are the school pictures all parents have of their children growing up. They then plaster them into photo albums, on the walls, in their wallets, and on Christmas tree ornaments. Pictures also get sent to all of the family members and to friends to remember the little angels forever, not wanting anyone to miss a single moment. Parents tormenting their kids for life is more like it.

———————

Kat just had her pictures taken and showed me the comb that all of the kids get beforehand. "They gave us these so we would all have nice hair for the pictures," she commented. About three weeks later they received their picture packets. Kat got on the bus, and showing me her pictures, said, "That comb wasn't very good. Look how my hair turned out!"

———————

A little boy looked at his school pictures with me. He wrinkled up his nose and asked, "Is this how I really look?" I smiled and said that it was a very nice picture. He studied me a moment and said, "Now I know why you wear glasses."

———————

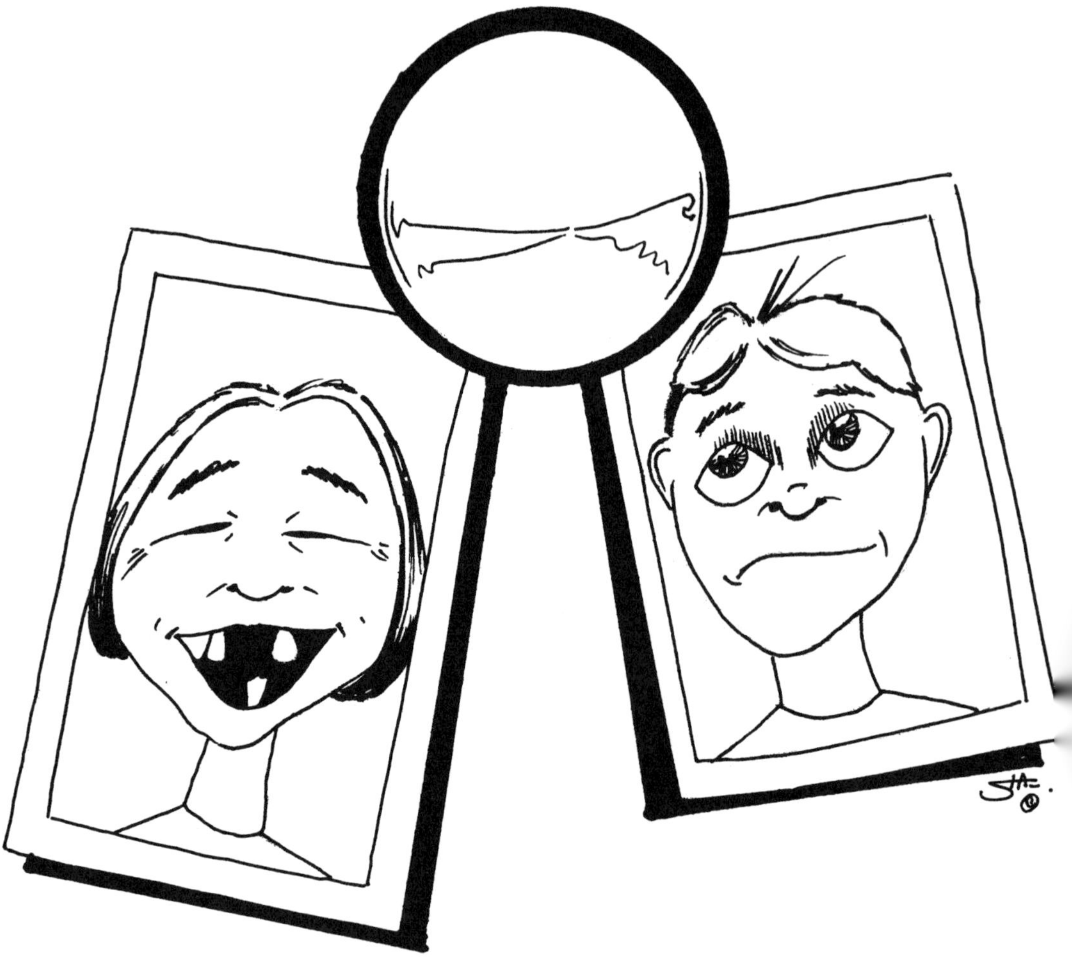

School Pictures

A sixth grader told me that her mother was going to have her school pictures redone. I said, "But your mom hasn't even seen these yet." "I know and she isn't going to. I am not going to have these follow me around for the rest of my life!"

One gal looked at her pictures and said, "That's not how I looked in the mirror before they were taken."

Tommy was really studying his school picture when he said, "Look how many teeth are missing. What was holding my mouth up?"

Andrew had broken his arm just before school picture time. His mother told him to make sure to get the cast into the picture. Three weeks later Andrew came to the bus very upset, showed me the picture, and asked, "Do you see anything wrong?" "Well, I see that the cast didn't show up, you're not smiling, and it looks like your talking to someone," I responded. "I know!" spouted Andrew. "I am trying to tell the man to get the cast in the picture!"

Do you remember when the boys went through the spiked hair-do era? At that time, I had one of the old buses where the seats weren't any higher than the kids' heads. I was driving along when I looked up into my mirror and all I saw were spikes; no faces just rows of over-moussed hair standing straight up.

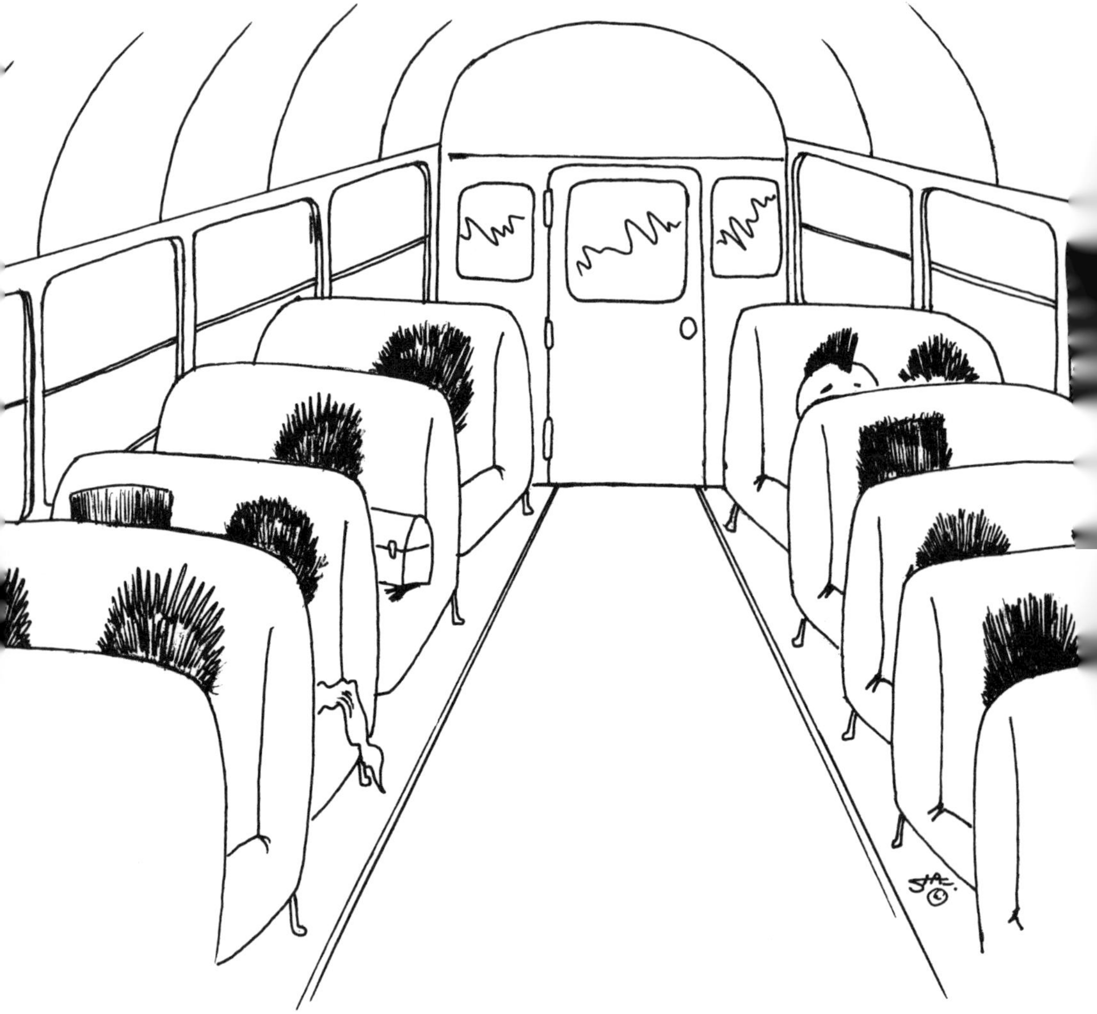

Love and best friends

Kids are not always sure what love is but they all think that they have it. Johnny, a four year old, insisted that he had to sit with Whitney every day because he liked her so-o-o-o much. The other day, he was so into playing with his new car that he didn't notice that Whitney had gotten off the bus. We were headed down the road when Johnny hollered out, "Where's Whitney? I was going to marry her today!"

One little boy told his girlfriend, "You have to kiss me and then we will be married." The little girl said, "But I don't want to marry you." Looking very shocked, he responded, "You have to! I already told my Mom!"

A couple of kindergartners were talking on the bus and the little boy said, "If we get married, you can live with me forever and you can share my toys." "Okay," said the little girl. "But only 'til we get to my house."

I overheard Missy, a kindergartner, talking to her best friend, Cindy, on the bus. She said that her mother was going to

I Live Next Door to My Neighbor

have a baby. Her dad said not to get her mom upset. A few days later Missy was very upset and told Cindy that she was going to break up with her boyfriend. "Why?" Cindy asked. Missy paused a few minutes and said, "I am pregnant." It's a wonder how a child's mind works!

Talking to a soon to be new brother, Troy, I asked, "What would you like your mom to have? A boy or a girl?" Troy looked at me and said, "Mama said that we don't care as long as it's wealthy."

I asked Andrew and Jazy how their mom was doing after having the baby. Jazy said, "Mom's tummy is smaller now that the baby is here." "Do you help take care of the baby?" I asked. "No, Mom feeds her the bottle and changes her diaper." Then Jazy looked at her brother and asked, "What does Dad have to do with the baby anyway?" "Are you kidding?" shouted Andrew. "He had to pay the hospital bill!"

Nick's grandpa came to the bus to pick him up. He was going to take him to the hospital to meet his new twin brother and sister. "What's their names?" I heard him ask. "Well," his grandpa said proudly, "Her name is Diane and the other is named after me." Nick jumped on the bus and shouted, "Did ya hear that Deb? One is named Diane and the other one is named Grandpa!"

Thomas had a pet gold fish that seemed to be his main topic of conversation day after day. He had even named the gold fish Sam. Well, like many goldfish before him, Sam died.

Love and best friends

Thomas got on the bus looking like he'd lost his best friend. So, in comforting him, I told him that his goldfish was up in heaven with God. Thomas looked at me very confused and said, "What would God want with a dead fish?"

Justin was sitting with Lacy when he decided to sit with Jacob, instead. Lacy got upset and said, "I thought that I was your best friend." Justin thought for a moment and replied, "You are, but I am not playing with best friends today."

Ty was about seven years old. He had been riding the bus for a couple of years and I had been his only driver. When I told him that I was going to leave and drive another route, he got off the bus crying. When his mom asked him what was wrong, Ty answered, "Deb is leaving." We tried to comfort him and he finally said, "You don't understand! She's been my driver for seventeen years."

Kids say and do

Stacy had a lot of trouble leaving her mom and riding the bus. Every day when she got to the bus, she started crying and holding on to her mom. Her mom would give a weak smile and drive her to school. On the fourth day her dad brought her to the bus. He put her in the seat and left. When we got to school I had the kids applaud her for not crying and for being a good girl. This went on for several days. One day, after I let all the kids off, I noticed that Stacy was still in her seat. "What's wrong, Stacy?" I asked. She said, with a little tone of disappointment, "You forgot to have everyone clap for me today."

It was a cold winter day and we had some trouble when four-year-old Jacob brought his teddy bear to school. It seemed he was having a bad day and it was only getting worse. He had to be corrected by his teacher several times about the bear. Now it was his turn to get off the bus and he wanted to give his winter coat to his bear to wear. Jacob explained that his bear would get cold. So, Rene, a bus aide, put the bear into Jacob's coat, zipping the bear and him in together. The next day

I Live Next Door to My Neighbor

we asked Jacob where his bear was. He responded, "Oh, that troublemaker doesn't have school today."

We have had some very interesting field trips. One time the kindergarten class went to a great pumpkin patch. Each child received a cute, round orange pumpkin. That is, all but one little boy. Ted had what looked to be the rest of the pumpkin patch. Bigger must have seemed better. His face was quite red from wrestling his pumpkin to the bus, up the stairs, and into the seat. Once he sat down, he had a grin from ear to ear. When we arrived at the school, it dawned on him that he wasn't on the bus for home and that he had to wrestle the pumpkin once again. I asked his bus driver when she got back to school how it went with the pumpkin. She said that when she glanced in her rear view mirror, she saw Ted sitting on it, sizing up the driveway.

On another four-year-old trip we went to the zoo. Sounds like fun, but not exactly. This zoo was in Lansing, eighty miles away. There is not a song in the world that you can sing for that many miles. Because they were only four, they could ride a maximum of an hour before they needed a snack, a bathroom, and break to stretch. The goal of this task is they have to be able to do this all and be back on the bus in fifteen minutes. This was the plan, but in reality it took forty minutes. Another head-count and we were on our way. When we got to the gate at the zoo, we had to pay for everyone which meant another head count and a quick trip to the bathroom before going in. They had exactly forty-two minutes to see the entire zoo, but that was where the two kids per chaperon comes in handy. The chaperons grabbed the kids under their arms and trotting as fast as they

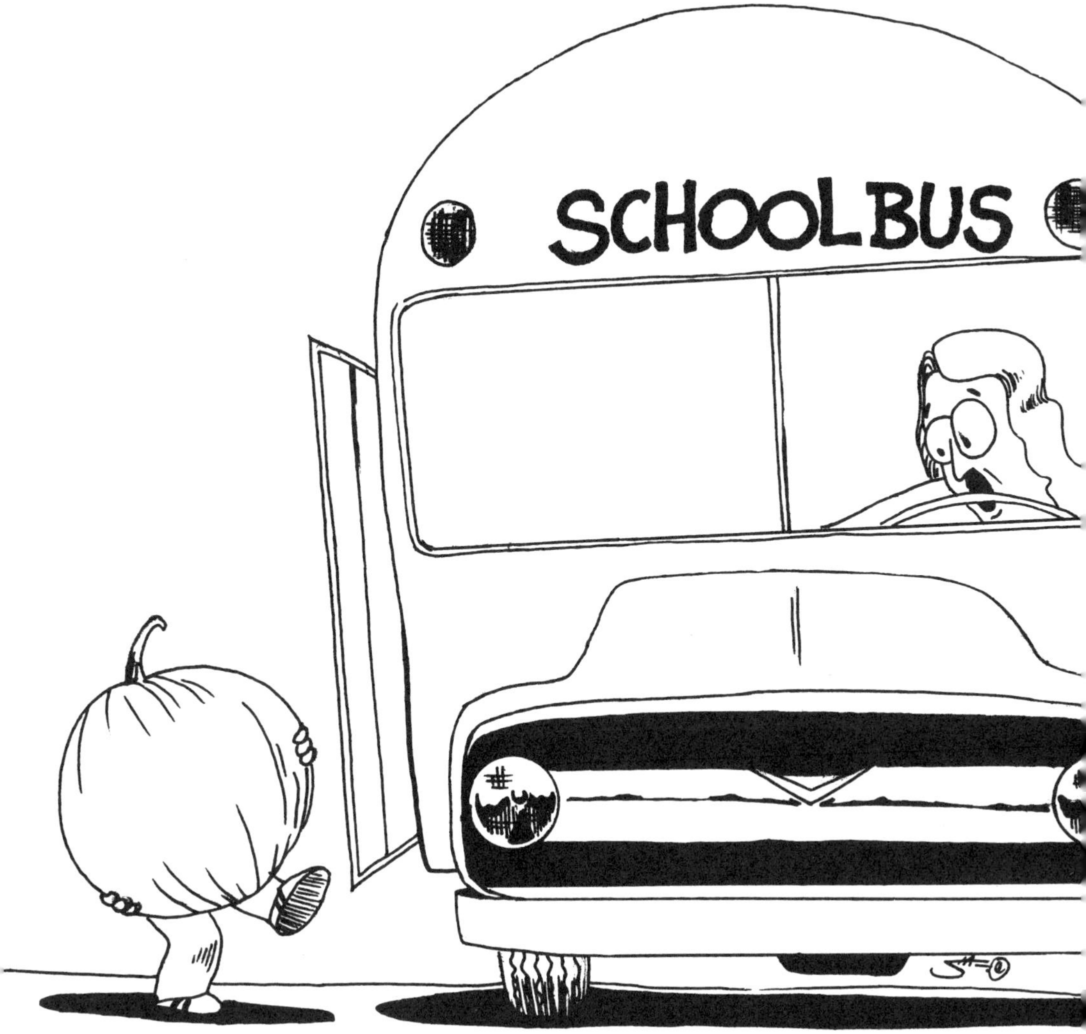
SCHOOLBUS

I Live Next Door to My Neighbor

could showed the kids the entire zoo. {Or, what ever they could see from that position}. Then everyone walked farther to get to the lunch tables than they did through the entire zoo. The kids ate and, of course, had to go to the bathroom. We did yet another head count and were on our way. One hour later, you guessed it, they needed a potty break and we did a head count. Ah, but by this time the chaperons had just about enough, so it went rather quickly. Looking into my mirror on the way home very few chaperons had their eyes open.

We were waiting at the unloading line to let the kids off at school. Tyler came up and tapped my shoulder. To my amazement, Tyler stood there with a large, flat lollipop stuck between his front top and bottom teeth, forcing his mouth to be opened to the limit. Not wanting to scare him, I smiled and said, "This just might catch on and be a new trend." Tyler pointed at his mouth as if I missed what the problem was. Of course I tried to remove it, but it would not budge one way or the other. Then his brother, Justin, came up to the front and offered to just pull it out. "No, I think we should be careful. It is in there pretty tight," I said, not wanting to cause a trip to the dentist or to give an explanation to his mother. Next, Justin took hold of the sucker and turned it, snapping it loose and leaving all the teeth where they belonged. What a way to start the morning.

When parents say things at home and little ears overhear them, they say to their children, "Now this is only for us to know about," "Don't you repeat this," or "Don't you tell anyone." Well, children do speak out and it usually starts with, "Mom said not tell anyone." I have tried to remind them of their promise,

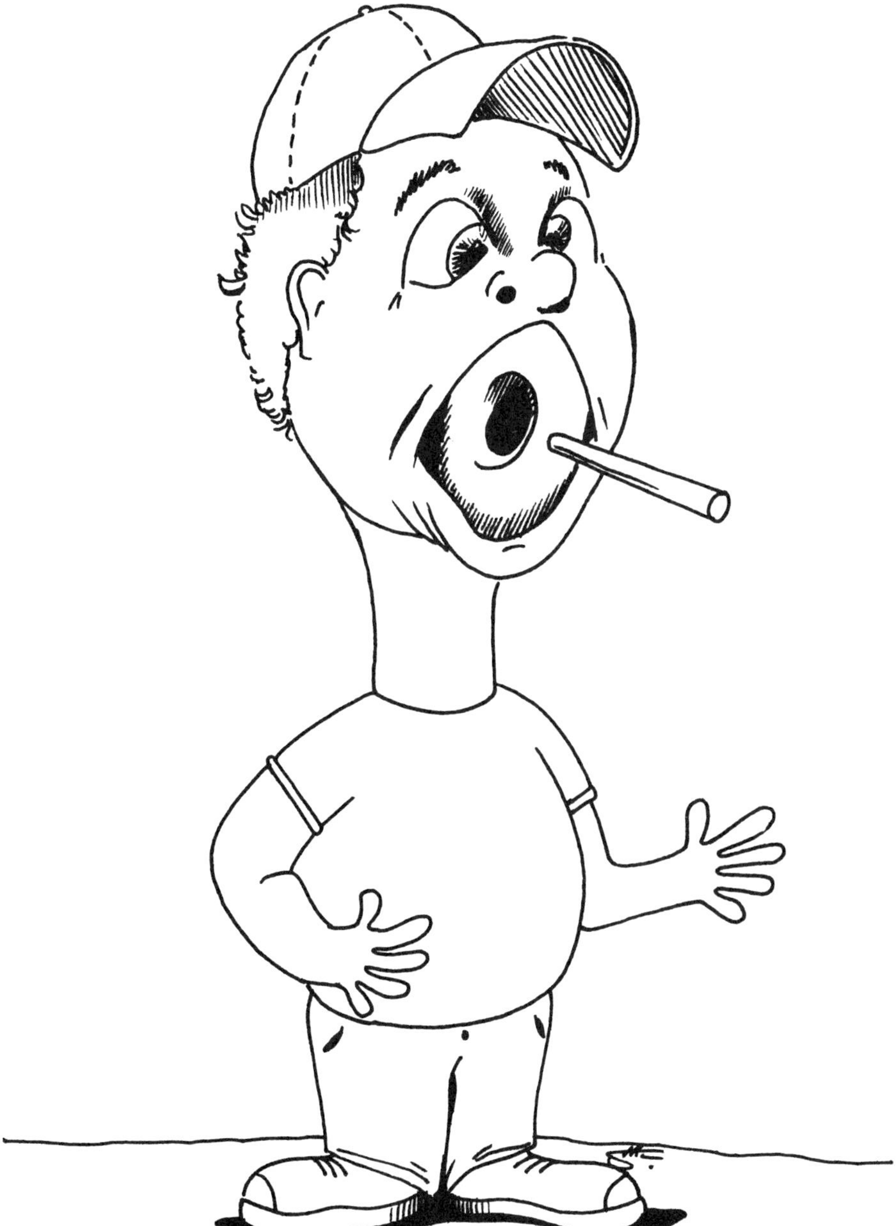

I Live Next Door to My Neighbor

but they seem to think that I am not the "someone" you meant. So one morning as we were driving by a large pumpkin patch, I mentioned that I still needed to get my pumpkin. One little boy said, "Well, we got ours last night." "It was too dark for me to get mine after work," I commented. He said, "Mom said not to tell anyone, but after dark we go over there and raid the pumpkin patch. If you want, I'll ask Mom to take me back tonight to get you one. It's real easy. We have been doing it for years."

T.J. wasn't in the habit of riding the bus in the morning. He lived next to his grandparent's place and was getting on the bus at their house. One morning they didn't call the school to say he was riding, but when I got close to his house, I could see a dim light flashing. I slowed down, and looking closer, I could see that it was T.J. He was flagging me down with a flashlight. I told him, "What a good idea that was, T.J." He said, "It worked better when I got the flashlight away from Grandpa." "Why?" I asked. T.J. responded, "Because Grandpa flagged down two cars and a truck before he let me do it."

T.J. would take so long to get to the bus at night that I was afraid he would miss his ride home. I finally asked him what was taking so long. He reached into his pockets and took out all kinds of things. He had a bottle cap, broken pencils, candy wrappers, and a single mitten. I asked him if he wanted to throw it away and he said, "Are you kidding? These are the best treasures I've found all week!"

A true farm boy explaining life on the farm told me, "Guess what? We had a calf born last night." "How nice! Was it a big

Kids say and do

one?" I asked. "Well, they're not as big as their mothers," he said. "Oh. Well, just how small was it?" I inquired. He leveled his hand about two feet off the floor and responded, "About tit high." So that's why those are down there!

───────────

Gaby rode my bus one night and told me that her cat had kittens. I asked her how many kittens she had. Thinking for a minute, she said, "Four: one red, one orange, one yellow, one green, and one black kitten." I then asked her, "What color was the mama cat?" "Oh," she responded, "she is all white." Hmmmm.

───────────

Julie, a fellow bus driver, came into the garage kind of snickering to herself. I asked her what had pushed her funny button. She said she had two little first graders, Amy and Sara, sitting in the front seat. Amy told Sara that her older sister got in trouble at home, and that her mom was very mad. Sara asked what her punishment was and Amy said, " I don't think she has one yet." "Well, I know what I would do," said Sara, "I would put her on the bus in the front seat for a week!"

───────────

Gaby asked me to do something with her. Teasingly, I told her that I couldn't because I was too old. "How did you get so old?" she asked. "Well," I explained, "I started out young like you and then I grew older. How did you get so young?" "Well, I wanted to grow up and I did," Gaby responded. "Hey!" I said, "That's how I ended up this old!" She looked at me for a second and pointing to herself, said, "I guess I was just lucky."

───────────

I Live Next Door to My Neighbor

Tommy found out that it was my birthday. He sang "Happy Birthday" to me, including the second verse, which asked, "How old are you?" When he finished singing, he was waiting for my answer. So I said, "How old do you think I am?" Tommy stopped smiling and asked, "How old do you want to be?" He must have been there before.

The first thing kids want to do when they get on the bus in the winter is to peel off all the clothes it just took their parents twenty minutes to put on. I had one girl, Jessica, who took off every winter item, including her boots. She then put on the shoes she used in the classroom. "Turn up the heat!" she shouted, "It's freezing in here!"

Muddy puddles

I was parked in the bus line waiting for the kids to come to the bus. It was raining and we had some large mud puddles near the buses. I sat in my bus watching the kids decide if they should go through or around the puddle. One little boy looked at his new shoes and then at the puddle. Then he held his foot above the water, closed his eyes, and stepped in. He looked over, saw me watching him, and looking shocked, he said, "I didn't even see that puddle there."

Several kids just ran through every hole that held water, the deep ones twice, splashing everyone in a four-foot radius before running to then next one. When they got to their bus, they told their driver that someone ran by a puddle and splashed them.

Kyle went up to the biggest puddle, "accidentally" threw his lunch pail in, looked around, shrugged his shoulders, and went in after it.

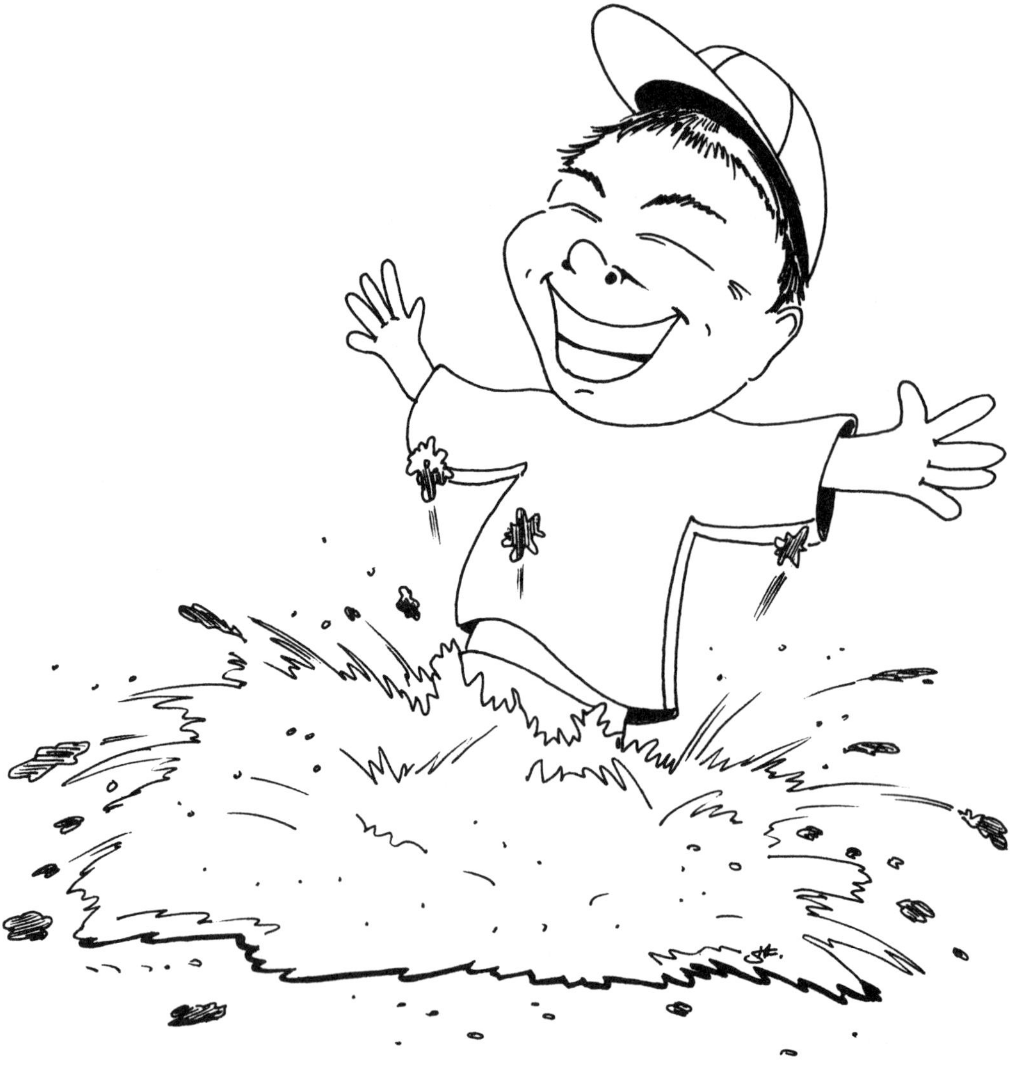

Muddy puddles

Another child, DJ, walked around the puddle several times before he jumped as high as he could and landed right in the middle of it with both feet, sending a spray of muddy water in all directions. Might as well do it right.

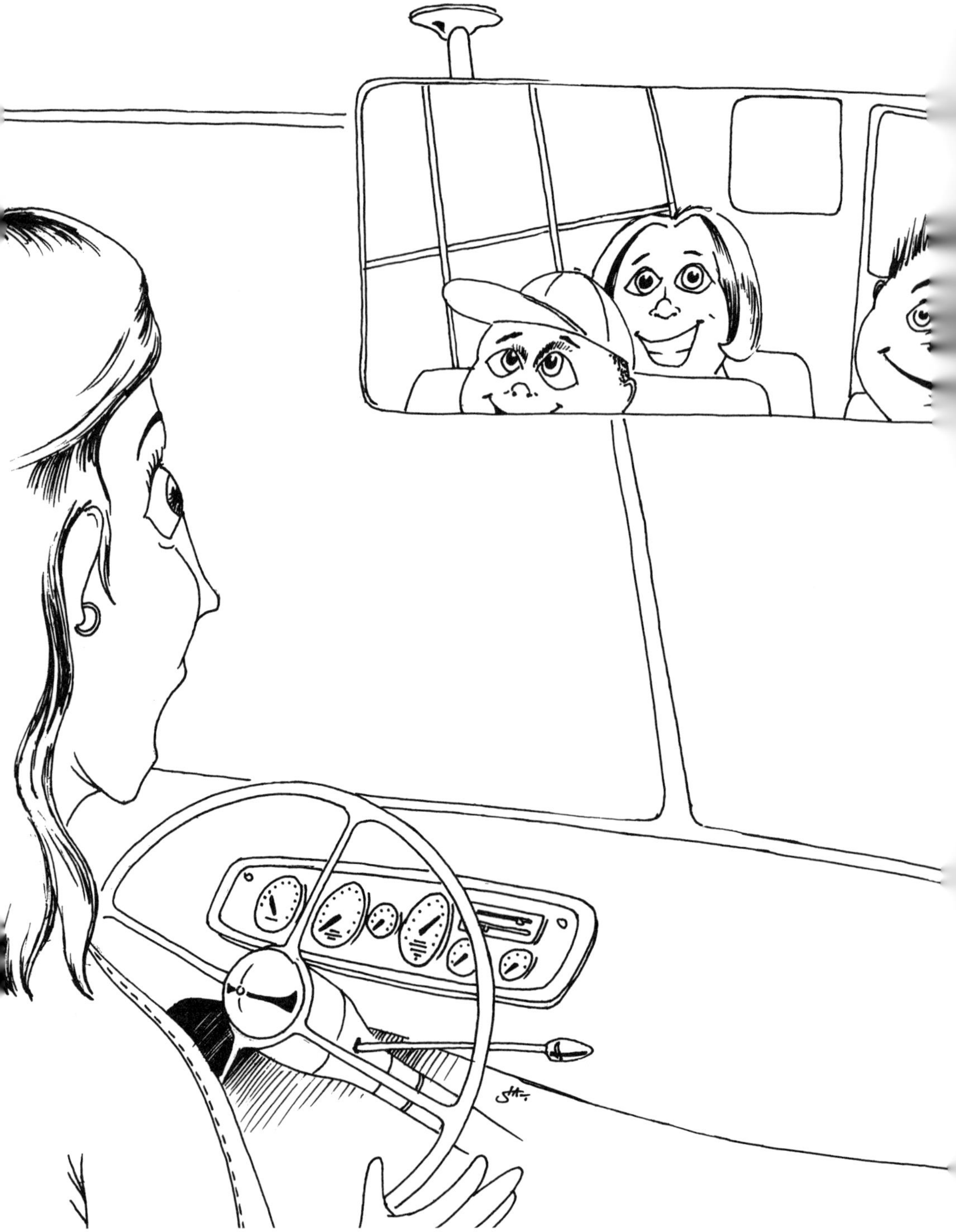

Slightly stressed

I'd like to take a few minutes to talk about a turnaround. A turnaround occurs at the last house on the road. Bus drivers use the driveway to turn the bus around. It sounds simple, but people plow their driveways the width of Volkswagon Bugs, and we try to back a 747 into them. We need forty acres to turn our buses around and what we get is forty seven inches. We also get an obstacle course of parked cars, kids' toys, bikes, garbage cans, pets, and ditches on each side. These are the houses we'd like to get a call from when the little darlings aren't riding the bus.

I had a very bad bus run one morning, which left me more than ready to have it over with. Usually, when bus drivers get the kids to school they drop them off at their buildings and park the buses at the bus lot. On this particular morning, I pulled in the lot, shut off the bus, and said, "Thank God that's over." Then I looked up in my rear-view mirror and to my horror I still had a full load of kids! Thinking that they had pushed me too far, not one so much as blinked. Not wanting to look like

I Live Next Door to My Neighbor

a total fool, I stood up and barked, "And we will park here every morning until you learn how to behave!"

Bus drivers learn to have a sense of humor the longer they have driven bus. I have been developing mine now for nineteen years and keep adding to it. I was very sick one day and had to go to the store for a few things. At the store I ran into a mother whose child had been on my bus at one time. I looked pretty bad and she asked me if I was all right. I said, "Yes, why do you ask?" "Well, you look pretty shaky," she commented. "Oh, that. It usually goes away in June," I responded.

I can't count the number of times people have told me that they could never do my job. Most of them are people with kids. Let's figure this out. I sit in front of sixty five kids with my back to them. They have seats that are higher than most of their heads, and over the noise of a diesel engine and heaters, I am suppose know what each child is saying and doing. As added excitement, on night runs there is generally a bit of a sugar rush going on. We have children ranging from preschoolers to twelfth graders on the same bus. Their moods vary from kids that are sleeping to kids that need to be peeled off of the ceiling. Bus drivers have to manage to keep their eyes on the road, know which children got on the bus and those who didn't, and keep the aisles clear of books and children, all while secured by a seat belt. Bus driving, what was I thinking?

There is also the fact that the bus is just so many feet long, leaving the students no place to go to escape one another's antics. Bus drivers get the, "He's looking at me." And, "He has

Slightly stressed

his hand on the back of my seat." Or, "Her things are touching mine," "She is drawing on my side of the window," and "I don't want to sit with him today." All of which simply means that more personal space is needed. With three children to a seat, kids are not going to get three feet of personal space. They're lucky to have a place to sit. The sooner this realization sinks in, the happier everyone will be. One minute bus drivers have these sweet little kids smiling and telling jokes the next they are like piranha's attacking each other.

Amidst all of this, while popping handfuls of Rolaids, the driver shouts, "Sit down! Get out of the aisle! Keep your hands to yourself!" Personally, I chew gum to control my stress. I can tell how tense my route has been by how sore my jaw is when I finally park the bus!

With anywhere from sixty-five to seventy students on a bus, it is not possible make everyone happy. For instance, when it's cold bus drivers will have the kids in one seat telling them to turn off the heat and the kids in the seat right beside them shouting to keep it on. The radio works the same way. There are kids who like rock music while others want country. Although they like each other's music, the two groups never want it on the same day.

Back packs

Parents must think that there is some kind of mitten-eating monster out there. On a daily basis we find single gloves, mittens, and hats that were left on the bus that morning. When bus drivers try to find the owners at night, no one has ever seen these items before. I usually display them for weeks on the bus. I ask kids who I think certain hats or gloves belong to and they take one look and say, "Nope." They can have their names written in them and the mittens or caps are still not theirs. "Is this your name?" I ask. "Yeah," they respond. I come back with, "Is this your hat?" "Nope," they insist. The two just never go together. One little girl, Jessica, had a very unique hat. When I tried to give it to her as she got off the bus, she just wrinkled up her nose and said, "No way." Just about every kid on the bus has a pair of those stretch gloves that fit every size. Hold a pair up and not one kid has ever seen them, not one kid. It's amazing. I am beginning to think that parents dress their kids and hide all of the mirrors.

I Live Next Door to My Neighbor

Backpacks should come with warnings on how big one should be compared to the size of the child. Hunter was a very small child and she had a backpack that a high school student couldn't carry. It looked like a full-sized suitcase. She dragged it beside her and had to hold her arm up next to her head in order to hold on to the handle. If it was on her back, anyone observing could only see two small feet and part of her head. The astronauts' life support wasn't that big.

The seats on a bus should hold three kids per seat. With luck a bus driver gets one and a half kids and two backpacks in one seat. Heaven forbid that the kids play sports or are in the band. Some kids carry a pack as big as what would be needed for a three-week vacation to Europe. Bus drivers spend more time finding places for the bags to sit than they do the kids themselves!

Book bags come in every size and shape. Most kids have back problems before they are in second grade. They haven't stood up straight since they bought their first backpacks. Take the time to peek inside a backpack. Beware. One boy was looking for something to show me and found a half-eaten cheese sandwich. It looked like he was growing his own penicillin. There were papers in there from the beginning of the school year. Shoes, boots, musical instruments, and anything that couldn't move on its own was in there. Go to any school bus and watch the kids. They get right up to the door and first thing they do is stop to take a long look at the three steps. Then they put their bags in front of them, grunt, head up the steps, and finally walk to their seats. Plop! They made it. By just putting down their book

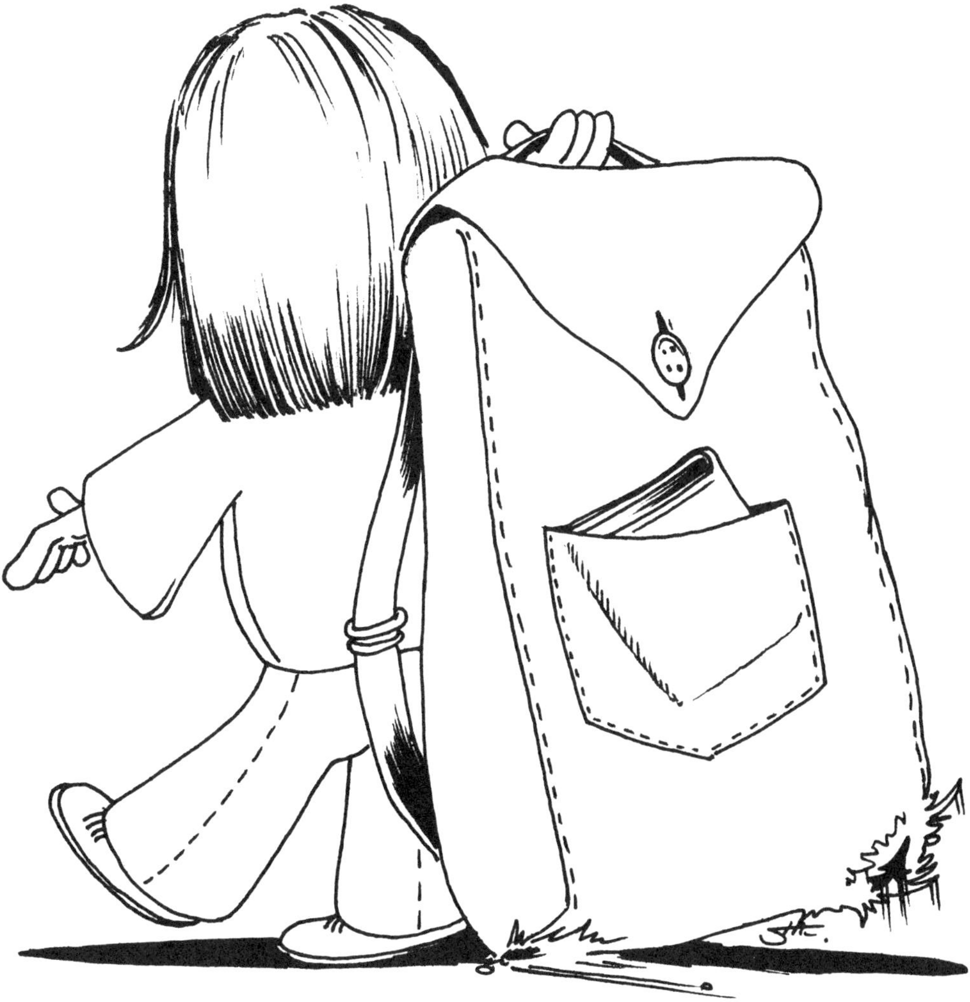

I Live Next Door to My Neighbor

bags, they are 20 pounds lighter. Then they come up to me and say, "I am dying of thirst. Do you have anything to drink?" "Well," I respond. "Let me see if I brought my garden hose today." Hmmm. They understand.

Conclusion

There are many more stories that could be told, and with school starting every September, the supply is endless. Each young child is willing to share his or her thoughts, feelings, opinions, and expertise on almost any subject. Kids tell their stories and talk about how they hear and see the world in the way that only children can. With a little patience, we can also find the humor in their stories. Know that children might not remember everything that you teach them, but they will always remember how you treated them.

Deborah Todaro Parsons

What is a School Bus Driver?

A school bus driver is a person who smiles in the morning and smiles in the evening and eats Rolaids in between.

A school bus driver gets there when nobody else can, finds houses that don't exist and children with no names.

School bus drivers have eyes in the back of their heads and hear every word, even in sign language.

School bus drivers are immune to noise.

A school bus driver's favorite words, {besides "good morning" and "good night"} are "sit down."

Sometimes a school bus driver gets tired, but seldom gets mad, and always, most faithfully, gets there.

{5-10-1999 Ann Landers}

A Bus Driver's Prayer

Please, Lord, watch over me this day. Please help me watch all five mirrors, two dozen windows, eight gauges, six warning lights, six dozen faces, three lanes of traffic, and to keep a third eye open for wobbling bicycles and daydreaming pedestrians, especially teenagers wearing headsets who are in another world.

Please, Lord, help me hear all train whistles, truck and automobile horns, police sirens and the two-way radio.

Please, Lord, give me a hand for the gear lever, the steering wheel, the route book, the radio microphone and the turn signal lever.

And, Lord, please grant me the self-control to keep my hands away from Johnny's neck. And one more thing, dear Lord, please don't let Mary be sick all over the bus.

And finally, Lord please watch over us all so that we can do it again next year. Amen

Ann Landers, author unknown

Order Information

Telephone Orders: Call Burdock Acres at (517) 386-3949.

To request books over e-mail: dktodaro@yahoo.com
Please leave an address and phone number.

Postal Orders:	Burdock Acres
		11023 N Whiteville
		Farwell, MI 48622

Please send $10.95 plus $3.00 shipping and handling.
Discount for quantity orders will be available.

Name: _____

Address: _____

City: _____

State: _____Zip:_____

Telephone: _____

e-mailaddress: _____